SPRINGBOARDS TO CREATIVE THINKING

101 Ready-to-Use Activities for Grades 3–8

Patricia Tyler Muncy

Illustrated by Janice Mori Gallagher

The Center for Applied Research in Education, Inc.
West Nyack, New York 10995

© 1985 by

The Center for Applied
Research in Education, Inc.
West Nyack, New York 10995

10   9   8

Library of Congress Cataloging in Publication Data

Muncy, Patricia Tyler
    Springboards to creative thinking.

    1. Creative thinking—Study and teaching—Handbooks,
manuals, etc.   2. Activity programs in education—
Handbooks, manuals, etc.   3. Language arts—Handbooks,
manuals, etc.   I. Title.
LB1590.5.M86   1985   372.13   85-11389

ISBN 0-87628-775-5

Printed in the United States of America

ABOUT THE AUTHOR

An experienced classroom teacher and remedial reading teacher, Patricia Tyler Muncy holds an M.S. in Education and is a Reading Specialist. She taught sixth grade for four years and remedial reading for five years. She has been a Reading Supervisor for the past eleven years, spending seven of those years as the Reading Supervisor for seven school districts in Wayne County, Ohio. She is also an Adjunct Professor for Ashland College in Ohio and has taught a number of graduate-level teacher education courses and workshops.

Mrs. Muncy is the author of a variety of practical teacher/learning aids. These aids include a teaching aid book, *Word Puzzles* (Belmont, CA: Fearon-Pitman Publishers, 1974); two instructional games, the *Froggie Alphabet Game* (Oak Lawn, IL: Ideal School Supply Company, 1976) and *Contraction Concentration* (Minneapolis, Minn.: T.S. Denison and Company, 1979); seven books of duplicating masters: *Word Play*, Books A and B (1977), *Handwriting*, Books A, B, and C (1979), *Dictionary Skills Grades 1 & 2*, and *Dictionary Skills Grades 5 & 6* (1980), all published by Instructor Curriculum Materials, Dansville, NY; and *Complete Book of Illustrated K-3 Alphabet Games and Activities* (West Nyack, NY: The Center for Applied Research in Education, Inc., 1980). She is also one of the authors of the Scott, Foresman and Company Spelling Program, *Spelling: Words and Skills*, Second Edition (1984).

For several years Mrs. Muncy has been conducting workshops in which she provides teachers with a variety of stimulating ideas for fostering students' creative-thinking abilities. A firm believer in the value of creative-thinking skills, she emphasizes the importance of teachers' purposeful encouragement and promotion of children's creative-thinking skills.

ABOUT THIS TEACHING RESOURCE

The purpose of *Springboards to Creative Thinking: 101 Ready-to-Use Activities for the Intermediate Grades* is to give teachers in grades 3 through 8 a store of ready-to-use activities to stimulate the development of creative-thinking skills in their students. This sourcebook is written in the firm belief that creative-thinking skills can be stimulated, developed, and enhanced through training. It is also written in the firm belief that *almost all* students can benefit from creative-thinking activities. While bright and gifted students need many opportunities and activities designed to develop and promote their creative-thinking skills, so do average and below-average students! Therefore, the activities presented here can be used in gifted classes but are also intended for use in the regular classroom with all students.

Each activity in the book includes a *student activity page* that can be reproduced as many times as needed and a *teaching suggestions page* that provides creative-thinking skill objectives, an activity introduction, sample student responses, as well as suggestions for follow-up activities. The teaching suggestions page precedes each student page and faces it, providing easy access to the suggestions for presenting the given activity.

Designed to develop the creative-thinking skills of *fluency, flexibility, originality*, and *elaboration*, the activities in this resource are varied, imaginative, highly motivating, and just plain fun! I hope you and your students alike find them highly beneficial and very enjoyable.

Patricia Tyler Muncy

CONTENTS

FANTASTIC CREATIVE-THINKING ACTIVITIES

Contents

REALISTIC CREATIVE-THINKING ACTIVITIES

Contents

HOW TO USE
THE ACTIVITIES EFFECTIVELY

Before you use the activities in this sourcebook, it will be most helpful to read this section. The following presents general suggestions that will help you and your students get the most out of the creative-thinking activities.

Specific teaching suggestions precede each student activity page. These include creative-thinking objectives, guidelines for introducing the activity, sample student responses, and one or more possible follow-up activities designed to further stimulate creative thinking.

SEQUENCE OF THE ACTIVITIES

The creative-thinking activities are *not* placed in a specific sequence in this book and do not require use in consecutive order. Instead, you have complete freedom to select appropriate activities for your class and to determine the order in which they will be used.

The activities have been divided into two general subsections:

FANTASTIC CREATIVE-THINKING ACTIVITIES — 58 activities dealing with pure fantasy

REALISTIC CREATIVE-THINKING ACTIVITIES — 43 activities of a practical, realistic nature

In your planning, you might select activities from one section or the other depending upon your purpose. Note that imagination can soar in *both* categories!

CREATIVE-THINKING SKILL OBJECTIVES

There are four major creative-thinking skills developed in this book:

Fluency: The development of a large quantity of ideas.
Flexibility: The development of a wide variety of different kinds of ideas.
Originality: The development of ideas that are original, unique, and unusual.
Elaboration: The development of ideas that exhibit the addition of much detail.

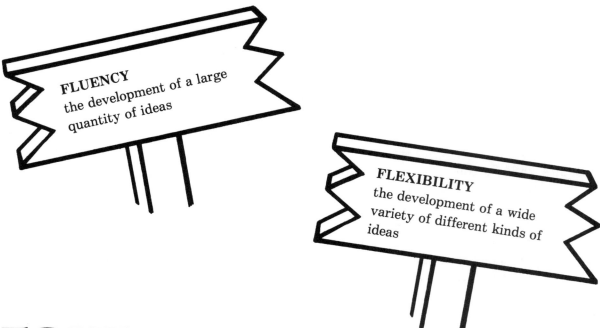

FLUENCY
the development of a large quantity of ideas

FLEXIBILITY
the development of a wide variety of different kinds of ideas

FOUR
CREATIVE-THINKING
SKILLS

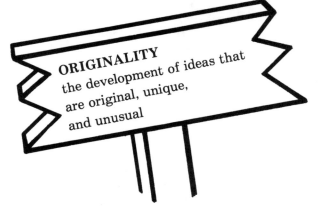

ORIGINALITY
the development of ideas that are original, unique, and unusual

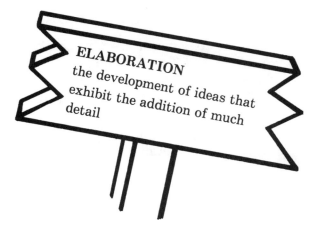

ELABORATION
the development of ideas that exhibit the addition of much detail

At the beginning of each Teaching Suggestions page the skills to be developed in the activity are identified. Some activities develop one major skill, but most develop three or all four of them. In some cases the Follow-Up Activities develop additional creative-thinking skills; these are noted in the list of skill objectives.

ACTIVITY INTRODUCTION

Provide Adequate Warm-up Activities to Stimulate Imaginations

After an activity sheet has been distributed to the students and the directions have been read and discussed, it is usually important to provide students with an idea-stimulating, thought-provoking, warm-up period. With most of the creative-thinking activities, students' imaginations should be activated *before* they are turned loose to develop their own ideas independently.

Here are three excellent warm-up techniques for frequent use in creative-thinking activities:

1. *Group brainstorming* — Invite the students to think of interesting and creative ideas appropriate for the particular activity and let them share those ideas aloud with the rest of the class as they think of them. Keep the pace lively to maintain interest and continuity from one idea to the next. This is an exciting, pleasurable, and highly motivating opportunity for the students to tell their ideas to you and their classmates. Many times the idea or ideas suggested by one student will serve as a springboard to new and exciting ideas for other students. Soon students will be eagerly raising their hands to be acknowledged, supercharged with wonderful ideas. Maintain order by insisting that students offer ideas only when called on. In this way, each student's contribution can be heard and reacted to.

Respond enthusiastically to each student idea with verbal and nonverbal acceptance and appreciation. Do not permit students at any time to make fun of or criticize the idea of another student.

After some interesting ideas have been generated in the group brainstorming session and the students are popping with ideas, have them begin writing down their own imaginative ideas on their papers as they continue to develop more and more ideas independently.

2. *Brainstorming in small groups or in pairs* — Have the students brainstorm in small groups or in pairs. This can be an interesting variation to large-group or whole-class brainstorming as a creative-thinking warm-up activity. Students can simply sit in small groups and share their ideas orally within their groups.

3. *Volunteer samples* — To get ideas flowing, give the students a few minutes to independently think and then write down some ideas for the particular activity. Then provide an opportunity for the students to volunteer to read some of the ideas from their papers. This oral sharing of ideas will stimulate the flow of new and different ideas as the pupils go back to working independently, developing different ideas from those shared aloud.

Provide Time to Work on the Activity

Whenever possible, give your pupils class time to work on the creative-thinking activity. At the very least, provide class time for them to begin jotting down a number of ideas while their imaginations are still charged from the warm-up activity. Then, if they must finish the activity at a later time, they will be more motivated and more successful in picking up threads of ideas to develop.

Since the creative-thinking activities are reading and thinking related, and help develop oral and written skills, you may find time during reading and language arts periods to provide students with opportunities to work on them.

Provide Motivating Responses as Pupils Work on an Activity

As pupils work on developing ideas in a creative-thinking activity, walk around the room pausing here and there to read ideas and to make appreciative remarks. Typical comments might include:

"I like the ideas you're coming up with."
"Wow! That's an interesting way of looking at it!"
"What a long list you've developed. Keep going!"
"That's a great list of ideas. Keep them coming!"
"My, you're off to a good start!"

This kind of sincere, encouraging response to their efforts keeps students motivated and encourages them to strive to develop more and more ideas.

And, while there are no wrong answers in a creative-thinking activity and all ideas should be received with acceptance, a critically important ground rule must be firmly established:

All students must clearly understand that rude, cruel, or off-color ideas will not be tolerated at any time in any of the activities.

Nonverbal ways of showing appreciation of ideas being developed are also important. An appreciative smile, an encouraging nod, a delighted look, a chuckle of enjoyment, or even a glint of pleasure in the eye are just a few of the nonverbal ways by which you can further show approval of students' creative-thinking efforts.

Encourage Pupils to Develop a Specified Number of Ideas

Many of the activities in this resource specify a minimum number of ideas the students are to try to develop. The reason for this is that the first ideas written by an individual usually tend to be the more commonplace ones. The more unique and original ideas tend to be developed as the individual continues to stretch his or her imagination for more and more ideas.

As the pupils begin to work on an activity that gives a specific number of ideas to develop, explain that the first ideas will probably come rather easily.

Then the ideas will start coming more slowly and with more difficulty. But emphasize that even though the ideas start to come more slowly, you want them to continue thinking of more ideas. Point out that many times the very best ideas are the ones developed when they start coming with some difficulty and require more thought.

Tell the students that the suggested number of ideas is simply a *target* toward which they should strive. Encourage them to try to reach the target, but never criticize them for failure to reach it.

SAMPLE STUDENT RESPONSES

If students have difficulty developing ideas in the warm-up session prior to working independently on the activity, use the examples given in the Sample Student Responses section of the Teaching Suggestions page to get ideas started.

FOLLOW-UP ACTIVITIES

Provide Opportunities for Sharing Favorite Ideas Developed During a Creative-Thinking Activity

It is important to give the students an opportunity to share favorite ideas from their papers. This sharing of ideas serves to further stimulate students' imaginations and helps them become aware of the wide range of idea possibilities. It also provides students with a rewarding opportunity to tell an appreciative audience some of the ideas they have developed.

Here are some techniques you might use for idea-sharing:

1. *Oral sharing of ideas* — Most of the activities in this sourcebook lend themselves to an oral sharing of ideas developed. The following guidelines will help make oral sharing a stimulating and exciting follow-up activity.

a. Place the oral sharing of ideas on a voluntary basis, as opposed to a "round robin" basis. In this way, students will willingly share ideas they have developed when they feel comfortable sharing them. It also avoids putting students on the spot when all of the great ideas they developed have already been given by other students who happened to have had the opportunity to speak first.

b. Limit students to sharing one or two favorite ideas at a time so that others who are excitedly waiting to share their ideas will quickly have their chance.

c. Encourage students to share with the rest of the class only those ideas that are different from those already presented.

d. Make the sharing of ideas a relaxing and pleasurable time in which students enjoy one another's ideas and laugh together over the humorous ideas that are bound to be developed in many of the activities.

e. Receive all ideas with verbal or nonverbal acceptance. There are *no wrong answers* in a creative-thinking activity.

2. *Other means of sharing ideas* — Some of the activities in this book best lend themselves to other means of idea-sharing. Sometimes the classes' completed activity sheets from one activity can be stapled into book form for leisurely enjoyment by individuals. At other times the end products of the activities lend themselves to displays such as bulletin boards, wall displays, or mobiles. Ideas from activities might also be shared in physically active ways like role-playing. Try brainstorming with your class to discover other interesting ways of sharing ideas.

Some sharing possibilities for a particular activity are provided in the Follow-Up Activities section of the Teaching Suggestions page.

Additional Ideas for Follow-Up Activities Are Provided for Many of the Creative-Thinking Activities

The teaching suggestions for some of the activities include a variety of creative-writing activities that provide further opportunities for elaboration of ideas developed during the original activity. Motivating and challenging follow-up activities of other sorts are also provided for stimulating variety.

Teacher Creativity in Developing Original Follow-Up Activities

While stimulating Follow-Up Activities are suggested for each activity, you should not feel in any way limited to the ones provided. Feel very free to develop additional or substitute activities as appropriate to the activity and to the needs, interests, and current areas of study of your group. Teacher creativity in developing new follow-up activities is definitely encouraged!

A Summary
of Effective and Ineffective
Instructional Techniques

$$\boxed{\textbf{WARNING}}$$

EFFECTIVE AND APPROPRIATE TECHNIQUE	INEFFECTIVE AND UNSOUND TECHNIQUE
1. Hand out activity page.	1. Hand out activity page.
2. Provide introduction of the activity directions.	2. Omit introductory discussion of directions.
3. Provide an activity warm-up session to stimulate imaginations.	3. Omit warm-up session.
4. Provide class time for students to at least begin work on the activity.	4. Assign activity to be completed independently entirely during free time.
5. Circulate among students as they work on an activity.	5. Sit at the desk or do other work while students work on the activity.
6. Provide an idea-sharing opportunity upon completion of the activity.	6. Fail to provide an idea-sharing opportunity upon completion of the activity.
7. Respond to all ideas developed with both verbal and nonverbal acceptance.	7. Collect activity papers to be corrected and graded.
8. Use additional follow-up ideas when possible.	

TROUBLE-SHOOTING SUGGESTIONS

1. **SAMPLE STUDENT RESPONSES** — If students have difficulty developing ideas in the warm-up session prior to working independently on the activity, use the examples given in the Sample Student Responses section of the Teaching Suggestions page to get ideas started.

2. **INAPPROPRIATE IDEAS** — While there are no wrong answers in a creative-thinking activity and all ideas should be received with verbal or nonverbal acceptance, a critically important ground rule must be firmly established:

   Rude, cruel, or off-color ideas will not be tolerated at any time in any of the creative-thinking activities.

3. **RIDICULE** — Students should not be permitted at any time to make fun of or criticize the idea of another student.

Establishing a Classroom Atmosphere
that Promotes Creative Thinking

Establishing a classroom atmosphere that promotes creative thinking is of prime importance for maximum success with the activities in this sourcebook. The following guidelines and suggestions will help you nourish the development of your students' creative-thinking skills.

Ready-to-Use Creative-Thinking
Posters and Bulletin Boards

At the end of the book, starting on page 223, seven creative-thinking poster and bulletin board ideas are provided in a ready-to-use format. These may be easily reproduced with an opaque projector by you or a student volunteer. Color can be added with markers, crayons, or poster paint. Display the posters and bulletin boards prominently in your classroom and you'll find your students chuckling as they get reminders to really dig for those supercreative ideas!

An Encouraging and Tolerant Atmosphere
Should Be Clearly Established

Make sure your students know that there are no "wrong" answers in a creative-thinking activity. All of the activities in this resource are open-ended to provide opportunities for development of a wide variety of novel ideas and solutions. The students must understand that there are many solutions to a problem. They also need to be encouraged to let their imaginations run free and to enjoy the wonderfully creative and original ideas they can develop!

In creative-thinking activities, students must feel safe from ridicule of their ideas. It is important to accept *all* ideas developed by the pupils regardless of how wild or even how common they may seem. You should carefully avoid any show of annoyance at any idea suggested. Instead, receive all ideas with appreciative comments and both verbal and nonverbal acceptance. Pursue any ideas you feel are hard to understand with leading questions.

Appreciative Comments and Relaxed Enjoyment
of Ideas Promote Creative Thinking

Whether brainstorming aloud together or sharing ideas after independent completion of an activity, the sharing of ideas developed in a creative-thinking activity should be a relaxing and pleasurable time. Students should respect and enjoy one another's ideas. And you should accept student ideas with warm, sincere enjoyment and enthusiastic comments.

Many of the creative-thinking activities in this book naturally lend themselves to spontaneous fun and enjoyment when the sharing of ideas takes place. Many times you and your students will find yourselves laughing together in pure delight over the humorous ideas sure to be developed. Appreciative laughter is rewarding to the students who developed the ideas and encourages the development of additional ideas. However, ridiculing laughter intended to mock a student's ideas must *never* be tolerated. Such ridicule will only cause the student to become highly reluctant to offer more of his or her ideas and will stifle imagination.

There Should Be No Grading of Creative-Thinking Activities

Make sure the students understand that the ideas they develop in a creative-thinking activity will not be corrected or graded. They should remember that there are no "wrong" answers in these activities, therefore their ideas cannot be graded. Instead of providing a source of grades for the gradebook, the activities give students the opportunity to open the doors of their imaginations and free them to soar to new heights without the fear of evaluation.

On occasion, you may wish to collect the students' papers to see how they are progressing in general and to look at the quantity and uniqueness of the ideas being developed. Be sure to let the students know the reason for your collection of activity sheets to avoid any fears of creative-thinking ideas being graded.

Students Need Opportunities to Share Their Creative Ideas

Students should have a variety of opportunities to share their creative efforts with others so they feel that their ideas are appreciated and the effort is worthwhile. Approving recognition is a tremendous motivator for students and encourages them to continued efforts in the future.

Opportunities to share their creative ideas can be provided in a variety of ways. Students can volunteer to share aloud with the rest of the group favorite ideas from their papers. Sometimes the activity sheets from an activity can be collected and bound to form a class book. Students can then read and enjoy one another's ideas; or students' favorite creative ideas can be developed into interesting bulletin board displays, mobiles, and murals, again providing students with opportunities to see and appreciate one another's ideas. Displays also give a satisfying feeling of accomplishment to the students.

One or more suggestions for student sharing of ideas can be found in the Follow-Up Activities section of the Teaching Suggestions page for each creative-thinking activity.

FANTASTIC CREATIVE THINKING ACTIVITIES

Teaching Suggestions for
ALL I WANT FOR CHRISTMAS IS AN ELEPHANT!

Creative-Thinking Objectives

Fluency
Flexibility

Activity Introduction

1. Distribute duplicated copies of the activity page.
2. Read aloud the activity instructions on the page.
3. To stimulate imaginations, have the students look at the illustrations along the border of the page. Then have the students read the two examples given on the student page.
4. Ask the students to think of and write down at least 18 more ideas during class time. Explain that the first ideas will probably come most easily. Then the ideas will start coming harder and slower. But emphasize that even when the ideas start coming more slowly, you want them to continue thinking of ideas until they have added at least 18 ideas to the page.

Sample Student Responses

(See the activity page.)

Follow-Up Activities

1. Let pupils volunteer to share some of their favorite ideas from their papers. Accept all ideas with appreciative comments and relaxed enjoyment.
2. Have the pupils circle the two ideas they like best on their papers.
3. *Bulletin Board Display:* Cover the bulletin board with attractive paper. Place the art on the following page under an opaque projector, project one elephant on the center of the bulletin board, and trace or draw the elephant. Add the title "WONDERFUL THINGS ABOUT AN ELEPHANT!" Next, have each student select two favorite ideas from his or her paper and write them neatly on 4½" × 2½" pieces of paper. Attach the ideas to the bulletin board so the students can read and enjoy one another's ideas.

Name _____

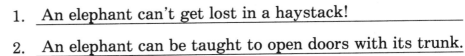

Think of all kinds of wonderful things about an elephant! Let your imagination run wild and come up with an elephant-sized list. Two examples are provided here to get you started! If you need more room, use the back of this page. List at least 18 of your own ideas.

1. An elephant can't get lost in a haystack!

2. An elephant can be taught to open doors with its trunk.

3. _____

4. _____

5. _____

6. _____

7. _____

8. _____

9. _____

10. _____

11. _____

12. _____

13. _____

14. _____

15. _____

16. _____

17. _____

18. _____

19. _____

20. _____

Teaching Suggestions for
PROGRAM THAT ROBOT!

Creative-Thinking Objectives

Fluency
Flexibility
Originality
Elaboration (Follow-Up Activity 4)

Activity Introduction

1. Distribute duplicated copies of the activity page.
2. Read aloud the activity directions on the page.
3. Let the students brainstorm aloud ideas of things they would like to program their robot to do.
4. After a number of the more common types of ideas have been generated, ask the pupils to begin thinking of some more unusual and original ideas of things the robot could be programmed to do.
5. After several more unusual and original ideas have been generated, tell the students that they are to begin listing their ideas on paper.
6. Explain that this will be a contest to see who can develop the most ideas of things to program their robot to do.
7. Allow class time for students to begin developing their lists of ideas.

Sample Student Responses

- Keep my brothers and sisters out of my room.
- Help me with my homework.
- Wash my dad's car for me.
- Guard our house from burglars.

Follow-Up Activities

1. Determine which student has developed the longest list of ideas. Check his or her list to make sure that there is not a duplication of ideas within the list. The student with the longest list is then declared the "Winner." Second- and third-place winners can also be determined, if desired.
2. Have the students read down through their lists and circle the three ideas they like best. Then have them underline the ideas they think are most original.
3. Let the students volunteer to share their favorite ideas orally and then their most original ideas from their papers.
4. *Creative Writing:* Let the pupils write stories about having a robot. Their stories might include how they got a robot, things the robot can do, interesting problems created by the robot, and so on.

Name _____

PROGRAM THAT ROBOT!

If you had a robot, what would you program it to do? List many interesting ideas and number each one. Be sure to include some ideas you think no one else will think of! Use the back of this page if you need more room.

Teaching Suggestions for
THIRTY IMAGINATIVE EXCUSES
WHY HENRY'S HOMEWORK ISN'T DONE

Creative-Thinking Objectives

Fluency
Flexibility
Originality

Activity Introduction

1. Distribute duplicated copies of the activity page.
2. Read aloud the activity instructions on the page.
3. Let pupils brainstorm some excuses for Henry's undone homework.
4. After a number of humorous and imaginative excuses have been suggested and chuckled over and imaginations have been stimulated, let the students begin writing down their own ideas of excuses independently.
5. Encourage the students to try to actually develop 30 excuses. If they are unable to reach that goal, accept whatever number they are able to develop.

Sample Student Responses

- He had his eyes examined the afternoon before and the drops in his eyes prevented him from being able to do his homework.
- While he was walking to school a thief snatched his notebook containing his homework and ran away with it.
- His brother mistook it for *his* homework and *he* took it to school.
- He was housetraining his puppy and the homework paper accidentally fell on the floor.

Follow-Up Activities

1. Have pupils circle the numeral in front of each excuse they think no one else would have thought of.
2. Let the pupils share aloud favorite excuses from their papers. This should be a relaxed and enjoyable time with pupils laughing together with enjoyment over the humorous excuses that are bound to be developed.
3. *Role-Play:* Have a small group of volunteers role-play Henry giving his excuses to his teacher and the teacher's responses.

Name _____

30 IMAGINATIVE EXCUSES WHY HENRY'S HOMEWORK ISN'T DONE...

Henry seldom has his homework ready, but he *always* has fantastic excuses for not having it done! He doesn't have it done again today.

Think of 30 possible excuses Henry can use to explain why his homework isn't done *this* time. The excuses can range from very believable to ridiculously unbelievable. Write your answers on a separate sheet of paper or on the back of this page. Include as much detail as you can.

Teaching Suggestions for
I CAN'T BELIEVE I ATE THEM ALL!

Creative-Thinking Objectives

Fluency
Flexibility
Originality

Activity Introduction

1. Reproduce the activity on a transparency or simply read it aloud.
2. Tell pupils they are going to have fun thinking up highly imaginative and humorous excuses for having eaten all of the wonderfully scrumptious cookies in the cookie jar.
3. Give the example provided as one possibility.
4. To warm up, call on students with ideas to share some of their ideas aloud. Accept all ideas given with sincere enjoyment and enthusiasm.
5. After five or six ideas have been shared, distribute duplicated copies of the activity page.
6. Ask the students to think of and write down on their activity pages nine more *new* ideas. Remind students that no idea is too farfetched!

Sample Student Responses

(See student activity page.)

Follow-Up Activities

1. Let students share aloud some of their favorite ideas from their activity pages.
2. *Ad Writing:* Have the students write and lay out an advertisement for a fictitious cookie company. They can make use of press-on lettering or words cut from magazines and newspapers. An illustration or magazine picture will add life to the ad.

Name _____

I CAN'T BELIEVE I ATE THEM ALL!

The cookie jar is empty! Every single delicious cookie has disappeared into your stomach! How will you explain this to your mother?

Think of nine different, highly imaginative excuses for eating all of those wonderfully scrumptious cookies!

1. Mom, I ate them all so you wouldn't be tempted to go off your diet! _____
_____

2. _____
_____

3. _____
_____

4. _____
_____

5. _____
_____

6. _____
_____

7. _____
_____

8. _____
_____

9. _____
_____

10. _____
_____

Teaching Suggestions for
GET THAT MONKEY DOWN!

Creative-Thinking Objectives

Fluency
Flexibility
Originality
Elaboration (Follow-Up Activity 2)

Activity Introduction

1. Distribute duplicated copies of the activity page.
2. Read aloud the activity instructions on the page.
3. Tell the pupils to let their imaginations go as they think of ideas. Tell them that the ideas they develop do not necessarily have to be realistic or practical.
4. Give the pupils adequate class time to develop and write down many, many unusual, humorous, and original ideas. Encourage the pupils to try to develop at least 20 ideas. Keep in mind that the first ideas that are developed are usually more the obvious and predictable ones. As ideas continue to be developed they usually tend to become more unique, more creative, and more original.

Sample Student Responses

- Park a truck full of bananas in front of the schoolhouse and entice the monkey down.
- Play a tape recording of a bunch of monkeys chattering and lure the monkey down to investigate.

Follow-Up Activities

1. Let pupils volunteer to share favorite ideas from their papers.
2. *Creative Writing:* Have the pupils write an original story to accompany their favorite idea generated in this activity. The story can be illustrated and bound into a book if desired.

Name _____

Imagine that you have a monkey act in a traveling circus and your star performer has climbed up into the bell tower of a schoolhouse *just* before showtime! How are you going to get that monkey down in a hurry?

List at least 20 interesting and imaginative ideas on another sheet of paper or on the back of this page. Provide as much detail for each idea as you can.

GET THAT MONKEY DOWN!

Teaching Suggestions for
NOW, *THAT'S A TALL TALE!*

Creative-Thinking Objectives

Fluency
Flexibility
Originality
Elaboration (Follow-Up Activity 2)

Activity Introduction

1. Distribute duplicated copies of the activity page.
2. Read aloud the activity instructions on the page.
3. To stimulate the flow of ideas, let pupils volunteer some highly imaginative, tall tale explanations of how the bedroom got so messy.
4. After some interesting ideas have been generated, tell the pupils that they are now ready to begin writing down imaginative ideas of their own.
5. Provide class time for the pupils to work on the activity.

Sample Student Responses

- The kids in my class are having a contest to see who can have the messiest bedroom and I plan to win!
- I had a wild dream last night and when I woke up this morning, this is what I found!
- The cat did this to my room!

Follow-Up Activities

1. Let the pupils share ideas from their papers.
2. *Tall Tale Writing:* Have each pupil select one or more of the ideas from his or her paper and develop the idea(s) into a highly imaginative tall tale about how the bedroom became a mess.
3. *Bedroom Illustrations:* Let the pupils draw pictures illustrating their versions of how their *own* bedrooms have looked at their messiest!

Name _____

Now That's a Tall Tale!

Your bedroom is a mess! Your mother is standing there with a scowl on her face wanting some explanation of why it looks like a disaster. Think up *many* highly imaginative, tall tale explanations of how your room got to be so messy. Number each explanation and use the back of this page if you need more room.

Teaching Suggestions for
SELL THAT HAUNTED HOUSE!

Creative-Thinking Objectives

Fluency
Flexibility
Originality
Elaboration (Follow-Up Activities 2 and 3)

Activity Introduction

1. Hand out duplicated copies of the activity page.
2. Read aloud the instructions on the page.
3. Have a volunteer read aloud the sample "sales pitch."
4. During class time, let the students work independently or in pairs to develop imaginative and perhaps humorous original "sales pitches."

Sample Student Responses

* This haunted house has several friendly ghosts to keep you company when you are alone and to entertain you with their noises and their tricks!

* **PRICE REDUCED:** A delightful old house, complete with creaking doors and ghosts. Buy now before this unique house is gone! Excellent rental possibilities to a major movie production company for use as the location for the filming of a movie.

Follow-Up Activities

1. Let the pupils share ideas from their papers. The pupils can then vote to determine which idea(s) they consider the most convincing, which idea(s) they consider the most original, and which idea(s) they consider the most humorous.

2. *TV Commercial Storyboard:* Have small groups of students collaborate to transform the sales pitches voted most popular into TV commercial storyboards. A storyboard consists of an illustration for each scene drawn within a TV-tube-shaped square with the script for the scene and any audio effects (music, sounds, and so on) written below.

SCRIPT:...
AUDIO:...

SCRIPT:...
AUDIO:...

SCRIPT:...
AUDIO:...

SCRIPT:...
AUDIO:...

3. *Role-Play:* The TV commercial storyboard in Follow-Up Activity 2 may be enacted through role-playing.

SELL THAT HAUNTED HOUSE!

Imagine you are a Realtor with a haunted house to sell! Think of a number of clever "sales pitches" you can use. One idea is given below.

Write your "sales pitches" on a separate sheet of paper or on the back of this page.

Example: "This haunted house represents a unique business opportunity! You can charge admission for guided tours of the house with guaranteed ghost appearances! This is an excellent buy for the investor who wants to get rich quick!"

Teaching Suggestions for
ONE CROSS CAMEL!

Creative-Thinking Objectives

Fluency
Flexibility
Originality
Elaboration (Follow-Up Activity 2)

Activity Introduction

1. Distribute duplicated copies of the activity page.
2. Read aloud the activity instructions on the page.
3. Emphasize to the pupils that they are to use their imaginations and that no idea is too farfetched.
4. Let the pupils work on the activity independently during class time. They should try to generate at least 20 ideas each.

Sample Student Responses

- Find another camel to keep it company.
- Have several truckloads of sand dumped in the backyard to make it feel more at home.
- Ship it off to the local zoo as fast as possible!

Follow-Up Activities

1. Let the pupils share ideas from their papers.
2. *Solution Illustrations:* Have the pupils each turn a piece of paper lengthwise and divide it into four boxes by folding it in half vertically, then unfolding and folding again horizontally. Next have each pupil select an idea from his or her activity paper and draw a sequence of four pictures to show the problem, the solution, and the result. Hang the finished solution illustrations on the bulletin board or on a wall so that the pupils can see and appreciate one another's ideas.

Name _____

ONE CROSS CAMEL!

Imagine that there is a cross-looking camel in your backyard. List at least 20 interesting ways that you could improve his disposition. Number each answer and use the back of this page if you need more room. Use your imagination!

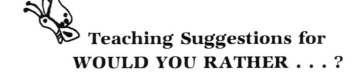

Teaching Suggestions for WOULD YOU RATHER . . . ?

Creative-Thinking Objectives

Fluency
Originality (Follow-Up Activity 4)
Elaboration (Follow-Up Activity 4)

Activity Introduction

1. Hand out duplicated copies of the activity page.
2. Read aloud the instructions on the page.
3. Have the pupils complete the activity independently during class time.

Sample Student Responses

I would rather be a butterfly . . .

• because I could flit from one pretty flower to another all day.
• because my wings would be so beautiful.

I would rather be a firefly . . .

• because I would like flying around in the dark all night.
• because no one would tell me to go to bed at night!

Follow-Up Activities

1. Ask the pupils who would rather be a butterfly to raise their hands. Then ask them to share some of the reasons why they would rather be a butterfly. Follow the same procedure with the pupils who would rather be a firefly.
2. Let the pupils discuss the disadvantages of being a butterfly and then the disadvantages of being a firefly.
3. Have each pupil make up two or three of their own WOULD YOU RATHER . . . ? questions. Then have pupils exchange their WOULD YOU RATHER . . . ? questions and answer one another's questions.
4. *Creative Writing:* Have the pupils each write a story about "A Day in the Life of a Butterfly (*or Firefly*)" from the point of view of the insect. The story should bring out the advantages of being that particular insect.

Name _____

Would you rather be a butterfly or a firefly? List at least ten reasons for your choice. Then make up some of your own "Would you Rather . . . ?" questions and give them to a friend to complete.

I would rather be a _____ .

1. _____
   _____
2. _____
   _____
3. _____
   _____
4. _____
   _____
5. _____
   _____
6. _____
   _____
7. _____
   _____
8. _____
   _____
9. _____
   _____
10. _____
    _____

Teaching Suggestions for
WHAT A PERFECT SPOT TO CAMP!

Creative-Thinking Objectives

Fluency
Originality
Elaboration (Follow-Up Activities 2 and 3)

Activity Introduction

1. Hand out duplicated copies of the activity page.
2. Read aloud the activity instructions on the page.
3. Let pupils work independently on the activity during class time allotted for that purpose.

Sample Student Responses

- On the top of Mt. Everest.
- At the exact location of the South Pole.
- On a beautiful, deserted South Sea Island.
- In a beautiful, huge cave that has stalagmites and stalactites and a fantastic underground lake.

Follow-Up Activities

1. Let pupils volunteer to share favorite ideas of camping spots from their papers.
2. *Creative Writing:* Have each of the pupils select one of their ideas of a camping spot and write a story about an exciting adventure he or she had on that overnight camping trip.
3. *Campsite Illustrations:* Let the pupils draw pictures of their chosen campsites. Encourage the pupils to include lots of detail in their pictures.

Name _____

WHAT A PERFECT SPOT TO CAMP!

Imagine that you have just won an overnight camping trip to any location in the world, with the camping equipment provided and all expenses paid. List and briefly describe at least 18 highly interesting and unusual places you would like to camp. Use the back of this page if you need more room.

Place a star by each of the five camping spots you think would be the *most* interesting. Compare your list with the lists of others in your class.

1. _____
2. _____
3. _____
4. _____
5. _____
6. _____
7. _____
8. _____
9. _____
10. _____
11. _____
12. _____
13. _____
14. _____
15. _____
16. _____
17. _____
18. _____

Teaching Suggestions for
STOP THAT SQUIRREL!

Creative-Thinking Objectives

Fluency
Flexibility
Originality
Elaboration (Follow-Up Activities 2 and 3)

Activity Introduction

1. Hand out duplicated copies of the activity page.
2. Read aloud the activity instructions on the page.
3. Let pupils complete the activity independently.

Sample Student Responses

- Put a screen over the chimney so the acorns can't be dropped down the chimney.
- Invite a dozen squirrel hunters to a picnic in your backyard.
- Rig up a noisy alarm system to go off as the squirrel approaches the chimney to scare it away.
- Hire the neighborhood kids to gather all of the acorns in the area and take them to the city park on the other end of town. The park squirrels would have a feast and the problem squirrel wouldn't have any acorns to throw down the chimney.

Follow-Up Activities

1. Let pupils volunteer to share favorite ideas from their papers.
2. *Creative Writing:* Have the pupils write an imaginative story of the situation from the squirrel's point of view.
3. *Ad Writing:* Have each student invent an imaginative device to keep the squirrel away from the chimney. Then have them write and illustrate a newspaper or magazine ad for the product.

Name _____

STOP THAT SQUIRREL!

Imagine that a mischievous squirrel has developed a game of dropping acorns down the chimney of your house. Think of many inventive ways to stop him from doing this. List at least 18 imaginative ideas. Use the back of this page if you need more room. Compare your ideas with those of your classmates.

1. _____
2. _____
3. _____
4. _____
5. _____
6. _____
7. _____
8. _____
9. _____
10. _____
11. _____
12. _____
13. _____
14. _____
15. _____
16. _____
17. _____
18. _____

Teaching Suggestions for
SUPER GIZMO

Creative-Thinking Objectives

Fluency
Flexibility
Originality

Activity Introduction

1. Distribute duplicated copies of the activity page.
2. Read aloud the activity instructions at the top of the activity page. Point out that the various parts of the gizmo have been numbered to aid in identifying the part of the gizmo they are referring to as they invent ideas of ways the various parts could be used.
3. Let the pupils work in groups of two or three to develop their lists of ideas. If the groups have difficulty coming up with ideas, have them think of ways a mechanic might use it, then how a gardener might use it, how a doctor might use it, how a zookeeper might use it, and so on, one category at a time.
4. After the groups finish developing ideas of uses for the invention, have the pupils return to their own seats and design an original gizmo on the back of the student page.

Sample Student Responses

Gizmo Part 1:   A tooth scraper for an elephant
Gizmo Part 2:   A tool for measuring the size of flower buds
Gizmo Part 3:   A seed planter
Gizmo Part 4:   A special paintbrush for painting stripes

Follow-Up Activities

1. Let pairs of students volunteer to share some of their favorite ideas from their papers.
2. *Bulletin Board Display:* Collect papers and hang them on the wall or on a bulletin board to display the student-designed gizmos for all to see and enjoy.
3. *Demonstration Speeches:* Have each student either illustrate or make a mock-up of their original gizmo and give a demonstration speech on its uses.

Name _____

Super Gizmo

How many ways can this new invention be used? Let your imagination go on an idea rampage! For each numbered gizmo part, list as many uses as possible in the numbered boxes below and use the back of this page if necessary.

On the back of this page design an entirely different and unique gizmo and list its uses.

1.

2.

3.

4.

Teaching Suggestions for
HOW TO GET AN OCTOPUS
OUT OF YOUR CHAIR

Creative-Thinking Objectives

Fluency
Flexibility
Originality
Elaboration (Follow-Up Activity 2)

Activity Introduction

1. Distribute duplicated copies of the activity page.
2. Read aloud the activity question on the page.
3. Call on volunteers to read aloud the two humorous examples given. Allow relaxed enjoyment and chuckling over the two examples.
4. Let pupils complete the activity independently during class time. As pupils work on their lists of ideas, walk around the room pausing here and there to read and enjoy ideas being written by the pupils. Expect pupils to develop at least 15 ideas of their own. Encourage pupils who wish to continue developing additional ideas.

Sample Student Responses

(See student activity page.)

Follow-Up Activities

1. Let pupils volunteer to share ideas from their papers. The sharing of ideas should be a relaxing and pleasurable time with students enjoying one another's ideas and laughing together with pleasure over the humorous ideas that are bound to be developed in this activity. Accept all ideas with verbal and/or nonverbal response.
2. *Comic Strip Writing:* Have each student choose his or her favorite solution in this activity and illustrate it as a comic strip. Balloons with the characters' words can be included if desired.
3. *Bulletin Board Display:* Create a display with the comic strips developed in Follow-Up Activity 2 above.

Name _____

HOW TO GET AN OCTOPUS OUT OF YOUR CHAIR

How do you get an octopus off your favorite reclining chair? Write at least 15 more ideas of your own. Use the back of this page if you need more room.

© 1985 by The Center for Applied Research in Education, Inc.

1. Lure it off with a bucket of its favorite kind of crabs. _____

2. Scare it off by dressing up as a giant squid! _____

3. _____

4. _____

5. _____

6. _____

7. _____

8. _____

9. _____

10. _____

11. _____

12. _____

13. _____

14. _____

15. _____

16. _____

17. _____

Teaching Suggestions for
NOW *THAT'S* INCREDIBLE!

Creative-Thinking Objectives

Fluency
Flexibility
Originality

Activity Introduction

1. Distribute duplicated copies of the activity page.
2. Read aloud the activity situation and directions on the page.
3. Allow sufficient time for pupils to develop their lists of at least 20 wonderfully incredible reasons. As pupils work on their lists of ideas, walk around the room, pausing here and there to read ideas and to make appreciative remarks.

Sample Student Responses

• I was just checking to see if a treasure map might be hidden in the vase.
• I was just trying to dust it inside and out.
• I was trying to catch the genie that popped down inside the vase.

Follow-Up Activities

1. Let pupils volunteer to share ideas from their papers. The sharing of ideas should be a relaxing and pleasurable time with students enjoying one another's ideas and laughing together with pleasure over the humorous ideas that are bound to be developed in this activity. Accept all ideas with verbal and/or nonverbal response.
2. *Vase Illustrations:* Have students draw X-ray pictures to reveal the insides of their vases.

You've gotten your hand stuck in a rare and valuable vase on your visit to the museum! List at least 20 incredible reasons for having inserted your hand into that vase. Write your answers on a separate sheet of paper or on the back of this page. Provide as much detail as you can for each idea.

Teaching Suggestions for
DRAW A CREATURE

Creative-Thinking Objectives

Originality
Elaboration

Activity Introduction

1. Pass out duplicated copies of the activity page.
2. Have a volunteer read aloud the activity directions on the page.
3. Have students look at the examples pictured on the activity page.
4. Let students create their own imaginary creatures, eight realistic and eight fantastic.
5. Allow students to use colored pencils or thick- and fine-line marking pens of assorted colors if they wish to add color to their creatures.

Sample Student Responses

(See student activity page.)

Follow-Up Activities

1. *Bulletin Board Display:* Create a bulletin board display with the completed student pages so that the students can enjoy one another's ideas.
2. *Creative Writing:* Have the students choose their favorite drawing and write an original short story or poem with the creature as the central character.

Name _____

Draw a Creature

Draw in features and details to make eight different realistic animals and eight different imaginary creatures. Make up a name for each creature and write it under the drawing. An example of each is shown below.

REALISTIC ANIMALS   **IMAGINARY CREATURES**

baby bird

wallfluret

Teaching Suggestions for
MAKE HER LAUGH!

Creative-Thinking Objectives

Fluency
Flexibility
Originality
Elaboration (Follow-Up Activity 2)

Activity Introduction

1. Distribute duplicated copies of the activity page.
2. Read aloud the activity situation on the page.
3. Give the students adequate time to write down many interesting and unusual ideas. Remind the students that the first ideas written down by an individual usually tend to be more commonplace. The more unique and original ideas tend to be developed as the individual continues to stretch his or her imagination for more and more ideas.
4. As students are writing down their ideas, walk around the class, casually reading some of the ideas students have written down, and making appreciative remarks and enthusiastic nonverbal responses to individual student efforts.

Sample Student Responses

- Spray laughing gas all around the room.
- Borrow Dumbo, the baby elephant, from the circus. When he starts tripping over his ears she's bound to laugh!

Follow-Up Activities

1. *Role-Play:* Select one girl in the class to play the part of the princess. Seat her in front of the class, facing the students. Let the students volunteer to share ideas from their papers. The "princess" listens to all of the ideas presented without comment. After a number of ideas have been given by the class, ask the "princess" to select one or more of the ideas that she thinks would have made her laugh.

    If desired, a second princess can be selected and more and different ideas can be presented by the class.

2. *Laughing Princess Illustrations:* Have the students select their favorite solutions from their lists and illustrate them. A bulletin board display can then be created if desired.

Name _____

MAKE HER LAUGH!

In all of her twelve years, the little princess has never, <u>ever</u> laughed. The king is worried about his daughter, so he has hired you to find a way to make her laugh.

List at least 20 interesting and unusual ideas to make the princess laugh. Write your ideas on a separate sheet of paper or on the back of this page. Provide as much detail as you can.

Teaching Suggestions for
THIS CALLS FOR ACTION!

Creative-Thinking Objectives

Fluency
Flexibility
Originality
Elaboration (Follow-Up Activity 2)

Activity Introduction

1. Distribute duplicated copies of the activity page.
2. Read aloud the activity situation on the page.
3. To warm up, let the students brainstorm aloud four or five possibilities.
4. Ask the students to try to think of 20 or more wild and wonderful ideas on how to get Santa out of that chimney.

Sample Student Responses

- Pour oil down the inside of the chimney and slide him out.
- Tie a rope around him and have a helicopter hoist him out.

Follow-Up Activities

1. Have students volunteer to share aloud some of their favorite ideas from their papers. Accept all ideas with obvious enjoyment and enthusiasm.
2. *Comic Strip Writing:* Have the students choose their favorite solution and illustrate it in a comic strip format. Balloons with dialogue can be used if desired.

Name _____

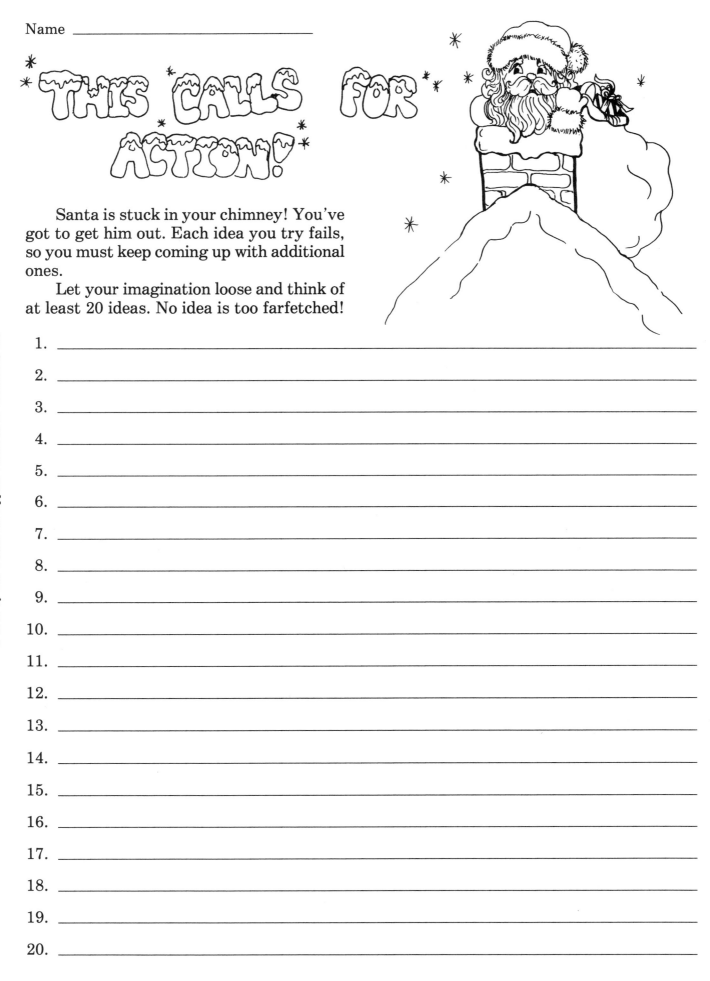

THIS CALLS FOR ACTION!

Santa is stuck in your chimney! You've got to get him out. Each idea you try fails, so you must keep coming up with additional ones.

Let your imagination loose and think of at least 20 ideas. No idea is too farfetched!

1. _____
2. _____
3. _____
4. _____
5. _____
6. _____
7. _____
8. _____
9. _____
10. _____
11. _____
12. _____
13. _____
14. _____
15. _____
16. _____
17. _____
18. _____
19. _____
20. _____

Teaching Suggestions for
PICK THE WINNING NAME!

Creative-Thinking Objectives

Fluency
Originality
Elaboration (Follow-Up Activity 2)

Activity Introduction

1. Distribute duplicated copies of the activity page.
2. Read aloud the activity instructions on the page.
3. Allow time for the pupils to complete the activity independently during class. As the pupils are working on the activity, walk slowly around the room, looking over shoulders to read ideas that have been developed and to sincerely compliment pupils on the ideas they are developing.

Sample Student Responses

- Super Sport
- Escape
- Speed Racer
- The Comet
- The Darter
- Zoomer

Follow-Up Activities

1. Write each student's favorite boat name on the chalkboard and then let the class vote by secret ballot for the name they like best.
2. *Ad Writing:* Have each student make a pasted-up layout of a newspaper or magazine ad for the boat using their favorite boat names. A boat photo or drawing can be combined with the students' original ad copy.

Name _____

PICK THE WINNING NAME!

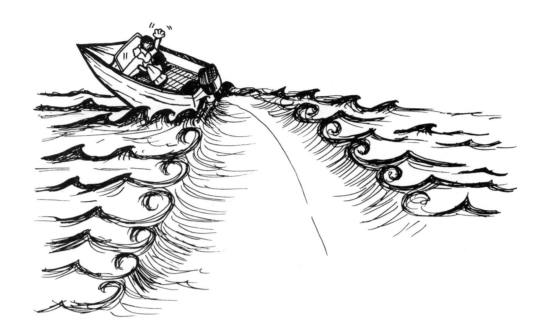

Imagine that the manufacturer of speedboats has just designed a small, very sporty, new racing boat. They are running a "Name the Boat" contest and the winner will get one of the beautiful, expensive racing boats plus $1,000 in cash!

You want to win the boat very much! Develop your list of at least 20 names, then circle the name you would submit in the contest.

1. _____   11. _____

2. _____   12. _____

3. _____   13. _____

4. _____   14. _____

5. _____   15. _____

6. _____   16. _____

7. _____   17. _____

8. _____   18. _____

9. _____   19. _____

10. _____   20. _____

Teaching Suggestions for
WHAT WILL YOU DO WITH A WOODS?

Creative-Thinking Objectives

Fluency
Flexibility
Originality
Elaboration (Follow-Up Activity 2)

Activity Introduction

1. Distribute duplicated copies of the activity page.
2. Read aloud the activity directions on the page.
3. Have the students read the two examples.
4. Provide class time for students to independently develop their lists of at least 13 additional ideas.

Sample Student Responses

(See student activity page.)

Follow-Up Activities

1. Let the students orally share ideas from their papers.
2. *Ad Writing:* Have each student select an idea from his or her paper and develop an interesting advertisement based on that idea. Drawings, photos, and press-on lettering can be combined with the student's original ad copy.

Name _____

WHAT WILL YOU DO WITH A WOODS?

Imagine that you have just been given 40 acres of woods with large, beautiful trees. Now, what will you do with that woods? Two ideas are given below to get you started. Provide at least 13 more ideas!

1. Organize a birdwatchers club and hold weekly meetings in the woods. _____

2. Build a lot of tree houses and rent them to kids in the neighborhood. _____

3. _____

4. _____

5. _____

6. _____

7. _____

8. _____

9. _____

10. _____

11. _____

12. _____

13. _____

14. _____

15. _____

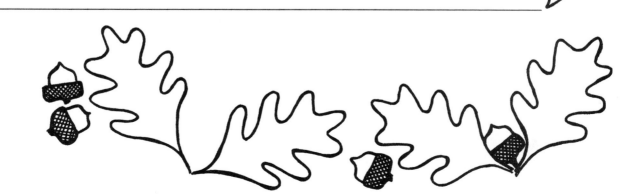

Teaching Suggestions for
THOSE UNWANTED RABBITS!

Creative-Thinking Objectives

Fluency
Flexibility
Originality
Elaboration (Follow-Up Activity 2)

Activity Introduction

1. Pass out duplicated copies of the activity page.
2. Read aloud the activity situation on the page.
3. To stimulate the flow of ideas, let pupils volunteer some ideas of ways to keep the rabbits out of the garden.
4. After some interesting ideas have been generated, tell the students they have heard only a few of the many ways that those rabbit could be kept out of that garden.
5. Tell the students that they are now ready to begin writing down interesting and imaginative ideas of their own. Have them try to generate at least 20 new ideas. As the students work on their lists of ideas, circulate around the room, casually pausing here and there to read ideas and make appreciative comments about them.

Sample Student Responses

- Buy a pair of foxes to patrol the yard and get rid of the rabbits.
- Install a noisy alarm system that goes off when a rabbit hops into the yard. The noise would frighten the rabbit away.

Follow-Up Activities

1. Let students volunteer to share some of their favorite ideas from their papers. Accept all ideas with appreciative comments and relaxed enjoyment.
2. *Editorial Writing:* Have the students write newspaper editorials on the rabbit problem. Before writing the editorials, have them examine a few actual editorial pages to get the feel for this kind of writing. Discuss the characteristics that set an editorial apart from other kinds of news writing.

© 1985 by The Center for Applied Research in Education, Inc.

Name _____

THOSE UNWANTED RABBITS!

Imagine that you are a person of great wealth with a beautiful home and garden. But you have a serious problem—rabbits are nibbling the gorgeous flowers and beautiful vegetables in your garden! You must stop those rabbits at once!

List below at least 20 really wild ideas where money is no object. Then compare your ideas with those of others in your class.

1. _____
2. _____
3. _____
4. _____
5. _____
6. _____
7. _____
8. _____
9. _____
10. _____
11. _____
12. _____
13. _____
14. _____
15. _____
16. _____
17. _____
18. _____
19. _____
20. _____

Teaching Suggestions for
WHAT A SWEET HOUSE

Creative-Thinking Objectives

Fluency
Flexibility
Originality
Elaboration (Follow-Up Activity 1)

Activity Introduction

1. Make a transparency of the activity page and project it with an overhead projector onto a screen. Or, place the activity page under an opaque projector and project it onto a screen.
2. Have the class as a group think of interesting disadvantages of living in a house made of chocolate candy.
3. As each idea is suggested, write it on the transparency or on the chalkboard near the screen. This is a time for relaxed enjoyment of the humorous and delightful ideas that are bound to be developed in this activity.
4. Continue the activity until at least 20 interesting and fun ideas have been suggested and written down.

Sample Student Responses

- It would attract ants.
- If you heated it in the winter, the walls would get soft or melt.
- Rats and mice would gnaw at it.

Follow-Up Activities

1. *Creative Writing:* Have the pupils write short persuasive essays on why houses should *not* be made from chocolate candy. While the pupils are writing, have the class-generated ideas projected on a screen or on the chalkboard so that the students can choose some of the ideas to elaborate upon in their writing.
2. *Bulletin Board Display:* Use the activity page as the center of a display around which you can mount the essays from Follow-Up Activity 1.

Name _____

WHAT A SWEET HOUSE

List at least 20 interesting disadvantages of living in a chocolate house. Be as inventive as you can!

1. _____
2. _____
3. _____
4. _____
5. _____
6. _____
7. _____
8. _____
9. _____
10. _____
11. _____
12. _____
13. _____
14. _____
15. _____
16. _____
17. _____
18. _____
19. _____
20. _____

Teaching Suggestions for
OUT OF THIS WORLD!

Creative-Thinking Objectives

Originality
Elaboration

Activity Introduction

1. Hand out duplicated copies of the activity page.
2. Ask the students to dream up imaginary creatures from outer space.
3. Each student is to draw a picture of his or her space creature in the area within the picture frame. Each of the creature's features should have a reason for its existence and placement. Pictures should be drawn with care and detail using colored pencils, crayons, or markers.
4. An imaginative name for the creature should be written on the designated line.
5. Students then write interesting and detailed descriptions of their creatures explaining the features and reasons for existence. Encourage students to proofread their creature descriptions to catch and correct errors and to make sure the description makes sense.

Sample Student Responses

(They will vary greatly.)

Follow-Up Activities

1. *Bulletin Board Display:* An enlargement of the UFO drawing on the activity page can be made using an opaque projector. Mount the enlargement in the center of a bulletin board and attach the student activity pages around it. In this way students can enjoy one another's ideas.
2. *Class Book:* Bind the student activity pages into a "Field Guide to Space Creatures" book. Use construction paper book covers and either punch holes for yarn binding or staple the pages together. Display the book so that it is available for students to read and enjoy one another's ideas. An upper-intermediate or junior-high class could also give the book to a third or fourth grade class to add to their classroom library.
3. *Newspaper Article Writing:* Have the students write newspaper articles describing the creature from outer space. Make sure to have them include the who, what, when, where, and why of the alien's appearance on earth in the first paragraph of the article.

Name _____

You have been the only witness to the landing of a UFO in your town! As part of your report on this happening, draw a picture of the alien from outer space in the frame below. Then write a paragraph describing its appearance.

Creature's name _____

Description of creature: _____

_____

_____

_____

_____

_____

_____

_____

_____

_____

Teaching Suggestions for
BE A BUTTERFLY!

Creative-Thinking Objectives

Fluency

Activity Introduction

1. Distribute duplicated copies of the activity page.
2. Read aloud the activity situation on the page.
3. Let students get into groups of two or three students and brainstorm together to develop their lists of ten additional ideas in each category.
4. Allow time for student groups to develop their lists. As students are working together, walk slowly among the student groups, stopping occasionally to listen to an idea being discussed or to look at ideas written down thus far. Praise student ideas and receive all ideas with positive comments.

Sample Student Responses

(See student activity page.)

Follow-Up Activities

1. Let student groups volunteer to share some of their favorite ideas from their papers.
2. *Creative Writing:* Have the students continue to imagine that they are butterflies and write their thoughts about the people who inhabit the world. The writing can take any form the students want—poetry, short story in the first person, newspaper interview with a butterfly, and so on.

Name _____

If you were a butterfly, how would you feel? What would you love to see and do? What would you fear? List at least ten ideas for each of these questions on the lines below.

WHAT WOULD YOU LOVE TO SEE AND DO?

1. I'd love to sip water from gurgling streams. _____
2. I'd love to investigate every flower in sight! _____
3. _____
4. _____
5. _____
6. _____
7. _____
8. _____
9. _____
10. _____

WHAT WOULD YOU FEAR?

1. _____
2. _____
3. _____
4. _____
5. _____
6. _____
7. _____
8. _____
9. _____
10. _____

Teaching Suggestions for
HOW DID YOU GET THAT SHINER?

Creative-Thinking Objectives

Fluency
Flexibility
Originality
Elaboration

Activity Introduction

1. Distribute duplicated copies of the activity page.
2. Read aloud the activity instructions on the page.
3. Have volunteers read aloud the two examples given on the activity page.
4. Emphasize that they are to think of at least 20 *really* imaginative and unusual ideas. Point out that getting hit in the eye in a fight is just too obvious an idea. Ask them to come up with far more interesting ideas.
5. Let the pupils work on the activity independently during class time.

Sample Student Responses

(See student activity page.)

Follow-Up Activities

1. Let pupils volunteer to share aloud favorite ideas from their papers.
2. *Black Eye Illustrations:* Let each pupil select a favorite idea from his or her list and draw a picture illustrating the event.
3. *Creative Writing:* Let the pupils write humorous poems about having black eyes.

Name _____

How Did You Get That Shiner?

You have a big black eye and all your friends are curious about how you got it! List at least 20 really imaginative ways to explain your shiner. Two examples are provided here to get you started. Write your ideas on a separate sheet of paper or on the back of this page.

Examples:

1. I was sleeping under an apple tree and an apple fell and hit me right in the eye!

2. I was fishing and had a big one on my line. As I was about to land the fish, it leaped

    out of the water and smacked me in the eye with its tail!

Teaching Suggestions for
ABSOLUTELY BURGLARPROOF!

Creative-Thinking Objectives

Fluency
Flexibility
Originality
Elaboration (Follow-Up Activities 2 and 3)

Activity Introduction

1. Hand out duplicated copies of the activity page.
2. Read aloud the instructions on the page.
3. Point out that the ideas do *not* have to be practical or realistic.
4. To stimulate imaginations, let pupils volunteer a couple of ideas for making a house burlarproof.
5. After some imaginative ideas have been generated, tell the students that they have heard only a few of the many possibilities for burglarproofing a house and that they should begin writing down 20 interesting and imaginative ideas of their own. Allow class time for the activity.

Sample Student Responses

- Install an elaborate burglar alarm system.
- Dig a moat around the house and put alligators in the moat.
- Invite Spiderman to move in as a permanent house guest.

Follow-Up Activities

1. Let the students volunteer to share some of their favorite ideas from their papers.
2. *Ad Writing:* Have the students work in pairs to create full-page magazine advertisements to sell imaginary burglarproof homes. Each ad should include the burglarproof features of the home, which may be selected from the activity sheet or the initial class brainstorming session. Students should use drawings or pictures along with original ad copy for the advertising layout.
3. *House Plan Drawings:* Have the students draw house floor plans with illustrations of burglar-detecting devices along with their placement.

Name _____

ABSOLUTELY BURGLARPROOF!

Imagine that you own a mansion and have unlimited wealth with which to make it burglarproof. Think of at least 20 really creative ways to do this. Let your imagination go wild!

Write your ideas on a separate sheet of paper or on the back of this sheet. Provide as much detail for each idea as you can.

Teaching Suggestions for
THE GOOD WITCH'S MAGIC BREW

Creative-Thinking Objectives

Fluency
Flexibility
Originality

Activity Introduction

1. Distribute duplicated copies of the activity page.
2. Read aloud the activity instructions on the page.
3. Have a volunteer read the example aloud.
4. Let two or three students volunteer more ideas of ways the brew could be used.
5. Allow class time for the students to complete the activity page independently.

Sample Student Responses

(See student activity page.)

Follow-Up Activities

1. Have students circle the numeral in front of each idea they think no other student would have developed.
2. Let students volunteer to share aloud favorite ideas from their papers.
3. *Creative Writing:* Have the students create their own imaginative, highly original recipes for a good witch's magic brew.

Name _____

The Good Witch of the West is brewing a kettle of her most powerful magic brew! Just a drop here and a drop there can make all kinds of good things happen!

How should the Good Witch use her brew? List at least 14 interesting ideas below.

1. Rid the world of mosquitoes! _____
2. _____
3. _____
4. _____
5. _____
6. _____
7. _____
8. _____
9. _____
10. _____
11. _____
12. _____
13. _____
14. _____
15. _____

Teaching Suggestions for
WHY RAKE LEAVES?

Creative-Thinking Objectives

Fluency
Flexibility
Originality

Activity Introduction

1. Distribute duplicated copies of the activity page.
2. Read aloud the instructions on the page.
3. Point out that the ideas do not have to be realistic or practical. Students should turn on their imaginations full blast!
4. Let the students brainstorm aloud together two or three imaginative ideas.
5. Then let the pupils work on the activity independently during class time. Have them try to develop at least 18 *new* ideas.

Sample Student Responses

- Have a firefighter with a firetruck hose them out of the yard.
- Have a helicopter hover over the yard and blow the leaves right out of the yard.

Follow-Up Activities

1. Let pupils share aloud favorite ideas from their papers.
2. As a class, let the pupils brainstorm aloud a number of ingenious ways of getting snow off of the sidewalk and driveway.

Name _____

WHY RAKE LEAVES?

Who wants to rake leaves? Develop a list of at least 18 highly inventive and unusual ways to remove autumn leaves from your yard . . . *without raking them!*

Write your ideas on a separate sheet of paper or on the back of this page. Provide as much detail for each idea as you can.

Teaching Suggestions for
GET THAT FLY!

Creative-Thinking Objectives

Fluency
Flexibility
Originality

Activity Introduction

1. Distribute duplicated copies of the activity page.
2. Read aloud the activity instructions on the page.
3. To stimulate imaginations, let the pupils brainstorm aloud some interesting ideas of how they could get that fly.
4. After some highly imaginative ideas have been offered, have the pupils begin developing their own ideas independently, writing their ideas on the activity page during class time.
5. Emphasize to the pupils that they are to try to develop at least 20 ideas. Point out to the pupils that the first ideas will come easily. Then the ideas will probably start coming more slowly and with difficulty. But emphasize that you want them to continue thinking of ideas even when it is hard.

Sample Student Responses

- Borrow the neighbor's fly-eating pet lizard.
- Dangle flypaper around the room.
- Chase it into my brother's room.

Follow-Up Activities

1. Let the pupils volunteer to share some of their favorite ideas from their papers.
2. *"Get That Fly!" Mobiles:* Have groups of five or six students each construct a mobile using the favorite ideas of the group members. The title "GET THAT FLY!" can be neatly printed on a 5" × 18" piece of colored posterboard and holes punched in the top for hanging. Each group member provides his or

her favorite idea with an illustration on a freeform shape cut from construction paper. A hole is punched in the center and near the top of each piece, and yarn of various lengths is used to attach the shapes to the title card. The pieces should be adjusted to hang in even balance. Hang the completed mobiles where students can read and enjoy one another's ideas.

Name _____

GET THAT FLY!

A very annoying fly keeps buzzing around you as you try to sleep! How are you going to stop that pesky fly? Use your imagination and list at least 20 really creative solutions.

1. _____
2. _____
3. _____
4. _____
5. _____
6. _____
7. _____
8. _____
9. _____
10. _____
11. _____
12. _____
13. _____
14. _____
15. _____
16. _____
17. _____
18. _____
19. _____
20. _____

Teaching Suggestions for
THE MAD SCIENTIST

Creative-Thinking Objectives

Fluency
Flexibility
Originality
Elaboration (Follow-Up Activity 3)

Activity Introduction

1. Distribute duplicated copies of the activity page.
2. Read aloud the activity instructions on the page.
3. To stimulate imaginations, let pupils share some ideas of ways invisible water might be used. Respond to ideas with positive comments and obvious enjoyment. Stress that no idea is too "far out."
4. After some interesting and imaginative ideas have been shared, tell the students they are ready to begin writing down their own ideas—the more imaginative the better.
5. Tell the students that when they have finished writing 14 ideas, they are to read and follow the directions at the bottom of the page.

Sample Student Responses

- It could be used to throw on an unsuspecting enemy.
- It could be used in water glasses on April Fools' Day.

Follow-Up Activities

1. Let students volunteer to share aloud favorite ideas from their papers. This sharing of ideas should be a relaxing and pleasurable time with students enjoying one another's ideas and laughing together over the humorous ideas that are bound to be developed in this activity.
2. *Bulletin Board Display:* Select a committee of students to develop a bulletin board display using ideas from students' activity sheets that the committee thinks are the most interesting and creative. The display could consist of an original drawing of the "mad scientist" or an opaque projector enlargement of the "mad scientist" art on the activity page with the students' ideas on strips of paper surrounding him. The committee should develop a title for the board and place it attractively.
3. *Creative Writing:* Have the students write imaginative stories using the story-starter phrase: *I drank the invisible water and suddenly . . .*

Name _____

THE MAD SCIENTIST

The mad scientist has done it again! He has made invisible water! Think of at least 14 different ways that invisible water could be used. Write your ideas on the back of this page or on a separate piece of paper. Provide as much detail as you can.

Think of two more inventions of the mad scientist and write them below!

1. _____

    _____

2. _____

    _____

Teaching Suggestions for
AN ELF FOR A FRIEND

Creative-Thinking Objectives

Fluency
Flexibility
Originality
Elaboration (Follow-Up Activity 2)

Activity Introduction

1. Pass out duplicated copies of the activity page.
2. Read aloud the activity situation on the page.
3. To warm up, let students brainstorm aloud four or five possibilities.
4. During class time instruct students to try to think of 20 or more wonderful things about having an elf as a good friend.

Sample Student Responses

- He'd have a terrific sense of humor and would always be playing tricks on me.
- He'd be so small he could sit on my shoulder when we go places.

Follow-Up Activities

1. Let students volunteer to share some of their favorite ideas from their papers. Collect papers, if desired, but make sure the students clearly understand that you are *not* collecting them for grading. Explain that you simply want to look at the quantity of ideas they have developed and enjoy the uniqueness of their ideas.
2. *Creative Writing::* Have the students interpret their lists of elf ideas by writing an original story with the elf as the main character speaking in the first person.

Name _____

Think about all kinds of wonderful things about having a tiny elf as a good friend. Let your imagination run wild and come up with a list of 20 or more ideas. Begin writing your ideas below and continue them on the back of this page or on another sheet of paper. Number each idea and provide as much detail as you can.

_____

_____

_____

_____

_____

_____

_____

_____

_____

_____

_____

_____

_____

_____

Teaching Suggestions for
STRANGE CREATURES

Creative-Thinking Objectives

Originality
Elaboration

Activity Introduction

1. Distribute duplicated copies of the activity page.
2. Read aloud the instructions on the page.
3. Have the pupils do the activity independently.

Sample Student Responses

(They will vary greatly.)

Follow-Up Activities

1. *Wall Display:* Collect the completed activity pages and display them on a wall so that the students can see and enjoy one another's ideas.
2. *Class Book:* On a sheet of unlined white paper, have each pupil write the name of a new imaginary creature, draw a picture of it, and write an interesting and detailed description of it. The creature's features should have practical reasons for their appearance and this can be explained in the description. Collect the completed papers and staple them together with a cover to form a class book. A title such as IMAGINARY CREATURE GUIDE BOOK should be printed on the cover. Place the book in a highly visible place and invite the pupils to take turns reading it during free time. After the class has had ample opportunity to read the book it can be donated to the school library or to the classroom library of a lower-grade class.

Name _____

Below are the names of four very strange creatures. From the name of each creature, decide what it might look like. Draw a picture of the creature, then describe it, telling the practical reasons for the way it appears. Tell what it eats and how it moves. Use the back of this page if you need more room.

SLIPSLOSH	GRICKLE-GRUFF

Description: _____
_____
_____
_____
_____
_____
_____
_____

Description: _____
_____
_____
_____
_____
_____
_____

MUGGLE-OOFF	BARBLE-GULP

Description: _____
_____
_____
_____
_____
_____
_____

Description: _____
_____
_____
_____
_____
_____
_____

Teaching Suggestions for
HIDE THAT MAP!

Creative-Thinking Objectives

Fluency
Flexibility
Originality
Elaboration (Follow-Up Activity 2)

Activity Introduction

1. Distribute duplicated copies of the activity page.
2. Enthusiastically read aloud the activity directions on the page.
3. Tell the students they are to think of and write down ideas of at least 20 highly unusual places to hide the map—places where no one else would even think of looking.
4. Provide class time for pupils to develop their lists of ideas.

Sample Student Responses

- In the squirrel hole in the oak tree.
- In a waterproof container in the toilet tank.
- Thaw a gallon of ice cream. Put the map in a watertight plastic bag, insert it in the melted ice cream, and then refreeze the ice cream.

Follow-Up Activities

1. Let the pupils orally share ideas from their papers.
2. *Creative Writing:* Have each pupil write an exciting story about the treasure map and the treasure, including how he or she found the map and what happened after hiding it.

Name _____

HIDE THAT MAP!

Imagine you have just found a real treasure map! Others know you have the map, so you must hide it. Where could you hide it? Think of at least 20 very unusual and imaginative ideas. Begin writing your ideas below and continue them on the back of this page or on a separate sheet of paper. Number each idea and provide as much detail as possible.

_____
_____
_____
_____
_____
_____
_____
_____
_____
_____
_____
_____
_____

Teaching Suggestions for
SUPER GUM

Creative-Thinking Objectives

Fluency
Flexibility
Originality

Activity Introduction

1. Hand out duplicated copies of the activity page.
2. Read aloud the instructions on the page.
3. Have volunteers read aloud the two examples.
4. Tell the students they are to really let their imaginations go wild in this activity. Emphasize that no idea is too farfetched! Remind students that their first ideas will probably come quickly and easily. Then ideas will come more slowly. However, they should continue developing ideas until they have added *at least* 18 ideas to the page.

Sample Student Responses

(See student activity page.)

Follow-Up Activities

1. Have pupils volunteer to share ideas from their papers. Accept all ideas with appreciative comments and relaxed enjoyment.
2. *Ad Writing:* Have the students choose their favorite ideas and use them to develop a magazine ad for the new gum. They should use photos cut from magazines or drawings, lettering cut from magazines or press-on type, and original copy for the ad layout. The finished ads can then be displayed on a bulletin board.

Name _____

The president of the largest chewing gum factory in the world has asked you to develop some new and very unusual types of gum. Help him with at least 18 of your own unique ideas! Two examples are given below.

1. Thinking Gum: It stimulates the brain and helps you remember better! _____

2. Freckle-Removing Gum: Chew a pack a day and freckles go away! _____

3. _____

4. _____

5. _____

6. _____

7. _____

8. _____

9. _____

10. _____

11. _____

12. _____

13. _____

14. _____

15. _____

16. _____

17. _____

18. _____

19. _____

20. _____

Teaching Suggestions for
TIGER ON THE LOOSE!

Creative-Thinking Objectives

Fluency
Flexibility
Originality
Elaboration (Follow-Up Activity 2)

Activity Introduction

1. Distribute duplicated copies of the activity page.
2. Read aloud the activity situation and instructions on the page.
3. Tell the students they are to really let their imaginations go as they think of some very interesting and highly unusual ways to get the tiger back into its cage. Emphasize that the ideas do *not* have to be practical.
4. Let the pupils work independently on the activity. Give the pupils adequate time to develop 16 unusual, humorous, and creative ideas. As the students are working, walk around the room, pausing here and there to read the ideas being developed and to make appreciative comments.

Sample Student Responses

- Call a fire truck and have the firefighters spray water at the tiger, forcing it back into its cage.
- Ask Tarzan to talk the tiger into quietly returning to its cage.

Follow-Up Activities

1. Let the pupils volunteer to share favorite ideas from their papers.
2. *Creative Writing:* Have each pupil select one or more ideas from his or her activity page to develop into an interesting newspaper article recounting how the tiger got loose and how it was replaced in its cage. Have pupils proofread their articles to make sure they make sense and to correct spelling, capitalization, and punctuation errors. Then display the finished articles on a bulletin board so that the pupils can read and enjoy one another's ideas.

Name _____

Tiger on the Loose!

A ferocious tiger has gotten loose from his cage at the zoo! It's up to you to think of some really unusual ways to entice him to go back. Write at least 16 different ideas and circle the ones you think no one else would think of. Continue your answers on the back of this page or on a separate piece of paper.

1. _____

_____

2. _____

_____

3. _____

_____

4. _____

_____

5. _____

_____

6. _____

_____

7. _____

_____

8. _____

_____

9. _____

_____

10. _____

_____

Teaching Suggestions for
MY INVISIBLE DOG

Creative-Thinking Objectives

Fluency
Flexibility
Originality
Elaboration (Follow-Up Activity 2)

Activity Introduction

1. Hand out duplicated copies of the activity page.
2. Read aloud the activity instructions on the page.
3. Tell the pupils they are to really let their imaginations go wild as they think of ideas.
4. Give the pupils adequate time to write down at least 20 interesting and humorous ideas. Remind the students that their first ideas will usually tend to be more commonplace. The more unique and original ideas tend to be developed as the individual continues to stretch his or her imagination for more and more ideas.

Sample Student Responses

Problems encountered because the dog is invisible:

- It startles and frightens people when it barks and there is no dog to be seen.
- The mail carrier constantly trips over the invisible dog sleeping on the porch.

Follow-Up Activities

1. Let pupils volunteer to share ideas from their papers. Accept all ideas with appreciative comments and relaxed enjoyment.
2. *Creative Writing:* The ideas generated in this activity lend themselves well to creative writing, either prose or poetry. Have each student select one or more ideas from his or her activity page to develop into an interesting and perhaps humorous short story or poem. The finished pieces can be displayed on a bulletin board for all to enjoy.

Name _____

MY INVISIBLE DOG

Someone has just given you an invisible dog for a pet! On another sheet of paper or on the back of this page list 12 problems you might have because your dog is invisible. Then tell about 12 interesting or funny situations you experienced with your invisible pet. Be creative and provide detailed descriptions of each idea!

Teaching Suggestions for
FIFTEEN WAYS TO USE A WITCH'S BROOM

Creative-Thinking Objectives

Fluency
Flexibility
Originality
Elaboration (Follow-Up Activity 2)

Activity Introduction

1. Distribute duplicated copies of the activity page.
2. Have a volunteer read aloud the activity instructions on the page.
3. Let students volunteer a few ideas to get imaginations charged.
4. Then let students work independently during class time to develop their lists of ideas.
5. Encourage students to develop at least 15 ideas. Students with more ideas should be encouraged to continue their lists.

Sample Student Responses

- It's a source of extra power when casting extrastrong spells.
- It provides a protective shield when she is in danger.
- It warns her when prowlers are approaching her cave.

Follow-Up Activities

1. Let students volunteer to share aloud their favorite ideas with the rest of the class.
2. *Creative Writing:* Have the students pretend they have found a witch's broom that is supercharged with magic powers. They then write highly imaginative stories of how they used the broom and what happened when they used it. When the stories have been proofread, corrected, and, if necessary, rewritten, they can be collected, bound into a book with an attractive cover, and displayed in a highly visible location. Invite the class to read and enjoy one another's stories at their leisure. This book of stories can then become a permanent part of the classroom library.

Name _____

Imagine that a witch's broom has *many* magical uses. What might they be? List at least 15 very unusual ways a witch might use her magic broom besides for flying. Begin writing your ideas below and number each one. Then continue on the back of this page or on a separate sheet of paper.

_____

_____

_____

_____

_____

_____

Teaching Suggestions for
THE BIG BAD WOLF SUCCEEDS!

Creative-Thinking Objectives

Fluency
Flexibility
Originality
Elaboration (Follow-Up Activity 3)

Activity Introduction

1. Hand out duplicated copies of the activity page.
2. Read aloud the activity directions on the page.
3. Ask the students to independently think of and write down at least eight interesting and imaginative ideas.

Sample Student Responses

- He could have pretended he was dying and when the pigs came out to see what was happening, he could have grabbed them.
- He could have hidden himself and waited patiently until the Little Pigs thought the coast was clear and came out to play.

Follow-Up Activities

1. Let students volunteer to share orally some of their favorite ideas from their papers.
2. *Bulletin Board Display:* Prepare a bulletin board display for your room or the school library. Cover the surface of the bulletin board with attractive paper. Then reproduce the picture of the Big Bad Wolf from the activity page by using an opaque projector to enlarge it for tracing. Place the Big Bad Wolf drawing in the center of the board and encircle it with students' favorite ideas written on 3" X 5" pieces of paper. In this way, classmates and other students can enjoy the ideas!
3. *Creative Writing:* Have each pupil select a favorite idea from his or her activity sheet and use it as the basis for writing a new ending for *The Three Little Pigs.* Volunteers can read their new endings for the class's enjoyment.

Name _____

THE BIG BAD WOLF SUCCEEDS!

The Big Bad Wolf did *not* catch the Three Little Pigs in the traditional story. Instead, he landed in the kettle of boiling water. Think of ways the Big Bad Wolf might have succeeded in catching the pigs! Begin writing at least eight different wily ideas below and continue on the back of this page or on a separate sheet of paper. Number each idea and provide as much detail as you can.

Teaching Suggestions for
HOW TO PUT OUT A DRAGON'S FIRE

Creative-Thinking Objectives

Fluency
Flexibility
Originality

Activity Introduction

1. Distribute duplicated copies of the activity page.
2. Read aloud the activity instructions on the page.
3. To get ideas flowing, let pupils brainstorm aloud a couple of imaginative ways to put out a dragon's fire.
4. Let pupils complete the activity independently.

Sample Student Responses

- Put a muzzle on the dragon's mouth.
- Shake sneezing powder around the dragon to make him sneeze so hard he will extinguish his own fire!

Follow-Up Activities

1. Let pupils volunteer to share favorite ideas from their papers.
2. *Idea Scrolls for Knights:* Divide the class into groups of three to four students each. Give each group a piece of 9" X 14" paper to decorate and roll like a scroll from the Middle Ages. Each group prepares a list of IDEAS FOR KNIGHTS ON HOW TO PUT OUT A DRAGON'S FIRE by selecting ideas from their activity pages and listing them on the scroll. The scrolls can be hung up on a bulletin board or a wall so that the groups can read and appreciate one another's ideas.

Name _____

HOW TO PUT OUT A DRAGON'S FIRE

You're a knight with a big problem —how to put out the flame of a fire-breathing dragon! Your countrymen are counting on you! List at least 18 interesting and unusual ways to solve the problem.

1. _____
2. _____
3. _____
4. _____
5. _____
6. _____
7. _____
8. _____
9. _____
10. _____
11. _____
12. _____
13. _____
14. _____
15. _____
16. _____
17. _____
18. _____

Teaching Suggestions for
SO *THAT'S* A WOBBLY!

Creative-Thinking Objectives

Originality
Elaboration

Activity Introduction

1. Distribute duplicated copies of the activity page.
2. Have a volunteer read aloud the activity instructions on the page.
3. Ask the pupils to draw the picture of the WOBBLY neatly, carefully, and with much detail using colored pencils, markers, or crayons.
4. In describing the characteristics of the WOBBLY, encourage the pupils to include as much detail as possible.
5. Let the pupils work on the activity independently during class time.

Sample Student Responses

- A newly invented riding toy for preschoolers
- A special walker for old people with wobbly legs
- A very special reclining chair designed to relax every muscle in your body
- A creature from the planet Zertroi

Follow-Up Activities

1. *Bulletin Board Display:* Collect the activity pages and display them on a bulletin board so that the students can see, read, and enjoy one another's ideas.
2. *TV Commercial Storyboard:* Have the students work in groups to create a TV commercial for a Wobbly that is a product. A commercial storyboard consists of an illustration for each scene drawn within a TV tube-shaped square with the script for the scene and any audio effects (music, sounds, and so on) written below.

Some groups may wish to actually perform their commercial for the class!

Name _____

What is a WOBBLY? Is it a creature? Is it a machine of some type? Is it a product? Is it a piece of furniture? Draw your interpretation of a WOBBLY and describe its characteristics in as much detail as possible on the lines below. Try to think of something no one else would think of!

Description: _____

_____

_____

_____

_____

_____

_____

_____

_____

_____

Teaching Suggestions for
FLY, BABY BIRD, FLY!

Creative-Thinking Objectives

Fluency
Flexibility
Originality
Elaboration (Follow-Up Activity 2)

Activity Introduction

1. Hand out duplicated copies of the activity page.
2. Have a volunteer read aloud the activity instructions.
3. Let the students work on the activity independently during class time.

Sample Student Responses

- Take it to the aviary at the zoo and let it watch the birds fly around. Maybe it will get the idea.
- Maybe it has underdeveloped wing muscles. Help it exercise its wings ten times a day.
- Sneak it into a bird nest with some baby birds who are about old enough to learn to fly. Maybe the mother bird will teach it to fly along with her own babies.

Follow-Up Activities

1. Let the pupils volunteer to share favorite ideas from their papers.
2. *Comic Strips:* Have each student choose his or her favorite idea and develop it into a comic-strip format showing the sequence of events. Colored pencils, markers, or crayons should be used. The finished comic strips can be displayed on a bulletin board or wall for the whole class to enjoy.

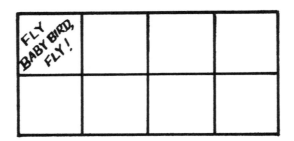

FLY, BABY BIRD, FLY!

Imagine that you found a baby bird on the ground two weeks ago. You fed the bird and gave it loving care. Now it is old enough to learn to fly, but it seems totally unable to do so. Each method you use to teach that bird to fly is unsuccessful, so you must continue to think of different and imaginative ways to teach the bird to fly. On the back of this page or on a separate sheet of paper list at least 15 different ideas of ways to teach your bird to fly. Let your imagination soar and provide as much detail as possible!

Teaching Suggestions for
SPECIAL DELIVERY PACKAGE

Creative-Thinking Objectives

Originality
Elaboration

Activity Introduction

1. Distribute duplicated copies of the activity page.
2. Read aloud the questions on the page.
3. To stimulate imaginations, let volunteers orally share some ideas of what might be in the box. Encourage students to turn on their imaginations and come up with some really interesting and unusual ideas.
4. After a number of interesting ideas have been generated, tell the students that they have heard only a few of the many possibilities for what could be in the box.
5. Tell the students they are now ready to reread the questions at the top of the page, write down their own interesting ideas, and tell about the situation.

Sample Student Responses

What's in the box?

- A small mummy straight from an Egyptian pyramid
- A vase with a genie
- A dozen crocodile eggs
- The camera from a space satellite
- George Washington's false teeth

Follow-Up Activities

1. Let the students volunteer to share their ideas orally with the class.
2. *Class Book:* Collect the completed activity pages and staple them together with a construction paper cover. Entitle the book "SPECIAL DELIVERY PACKAGE" and place it where students can read one another's ideas during free time.

Name _____

SPECIAL DELIVERY PACKAGE

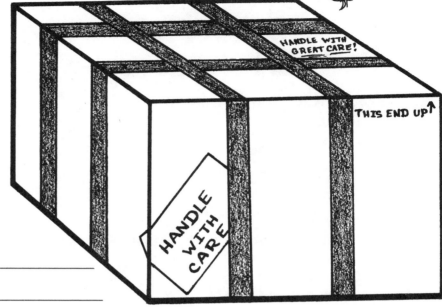

You have received a Special Delivery package! Really use your imagination to tell what is in the box, why it was delivered to you, and how you are going to use it!

This box contains:

_____

_____

It was delivered to me because _____

_____

_____

_____

I am going to use _____

_____

_____

_____

_____

_____

_____

_____

_____

_____

Teaching Suggestions for
IF I WERE A POLAR BEAR . . .

Creative-Thinking Objectives

Fluency
Flexibility
Originality
Elaboration (Follow-Up Activity 2)

Activity Introduction

1. Make a transparency of the activity page and project it onto a screen with an overhead projector. Or project the page with an opaque projector.
2. Have the class brainstorm some interesting ideas of what they would love to see and do and what they would fear if they were polar bears.
3. As each idea is suggested, either write it directly on the transparency or on the chalkboard near the screen if you are using an opaque projector.

Sample Student Responses

What would you love to see and do?

- I would like to stand on an iceberg and gaze at the northern lights.
- I would love to sniff the frigid Arctic air.

What would you fear?

- Being grabbed by a giant squid while swimming.
- Cutting my paw on a sharp piece of ice.

Follow-Up Activities

1. Have each of the students select one of the following topics. Using the same activity format, they should independently list on a sheet of paper ideas of what they would love to see and do and what they would fear if they were that animal.
   IF I WERE AN EAGLE . . .
   IF I WERE A SQUIRREL . . .
   IF I WERE A RACCOON . . .
2. *Creative Writing:* Have the students use either the ideas generated in the activity "If I were a Polar Bear . . ." or in Follow-Up Activity 1 above as the basis for either a short story or poem. The student should assume the role of the animal and write in the first person.

100

Name _____

IF I WERE A POLAR BEAR...

Imagine you are a polar bear! What would you love to see and do? What would you fear? Think of at least 10 really creative ideas for each question.

What would you love to see and do?

1. _____
2. _____
3. _____
4. _____
5. _____
6. _____
7. _____
8. _____
9. _____
10. _____

What would you fear?

1. _____
2. _____
3. _____
4. _____
5. _____
6. _____
7. _____
8. _____
9. _____
10. _____

Teaching Suggestions for
MARY, WHY DIDN'T YOU THINK OF THAT?

Creative-Thinking Objectives

Fluency
Flexibility
Originality
Elaboration (Follow-Up Activity 2)

Activity Introduction

1. Distribute duplicated copies of the activity page.
2. Read aloud the instructions on the page.
3. Emphasize that the ideas should be highly imaginative but not necessarily practical.
4. Point out to the students that when they have finished writing down their ideas, they are to follow the directions at the bottom of the activity page, giving careful thought to their selections.
5. Provide class time for the students to work on the activity independently.

Sample Student Responses

- She could attach a radar beeper to the lamb's collar. Then she could always locate the lamb when it wanders off!
- She could hire a babysitter to watch her lamb.

Follow-Up Activities

1. First let the students share the ideas they consider to be the most practical. Then let them share the ideas they consider the most original and creative. Ask the pupils to share only those ideas that have not previously been given.
2. *Lamb Illustrations:* Have each student choose his or her favorite idea and illustrate it using colored pencils, markers, or crayons. He or she should provide a short caption for the illustration to describe the idea. The illustrations may be used for a wall display or bulletin board so that the students can enjoy one another's ideas.

Name _____

MARY, WHY DIDN'T YOU THINK OF THAT?

Mary keeps losing her little lamb! Think of 15 unique ways to help her solve this problem. No idea is too farfetched!

Draw a circle around the number of each of the three ideas you feel are most practical. Then place a star in front of each of the three ideas you feel are most original and creative.

1. _____

2. _____

3. _____

4. _____

5. _____

6. _____

7. _____

8. _____

9. _____

10. _____

11. _____

12. _____

13. _____

14. _____

15. _____

Teaching Suggestions for
TALK, TURKEY, TALK!

Creative-Thinking Objectives

Fluency
Flexibility
Originality
Elaboration (Follow-Up Activity 2)

Activity Introduction

1. Distribute duplicated copies of the activity page.
2. Have a volunteer read aloud the instructions on the page.
3. Let the students volunteer a few ideas to get imaginations stimulated.
4. Then let the students work independently, developing their lists of at least 20 ideas during class time. As pupils are writing down ideas, casually walk around the room, pausing here and there to read an idea and to make an appreciative comment. This will keep the students on task and enthusiastically working on their lists.

Sample Student Responses

- I'd tell the farmer that I accidentally ate some corn that had been contaminated by an unsafe chemical and for his own safety, and for the safety of his family, he had better have roast beef instead of turkey this Thanksgiving.
- I'd tell the farmer that in a national opinion survey roast beef rated far ahead of turkey in food preferences. Therefore, his family really should have roast beef for Thanksgiving dinner.

Follow-Up Activities

1. Let students volunteer to share aloud favorite ideas with the rest of the class.
2. *Creative Writing:* Using ideas developed in the activity, have the students each take the role of the turkey and write a persuasive newspaper editorial to convince the public that turkey should *not* be served for Thanksgiving dinner. The completed editorials may be displayed on a wall or bulletin board, or bound into a class book so that the students may enjoy one another's ideas.

Talk Turkey, Talk!

Imagine that you are the Thanksgiving turkey about to be served up for dinner! How can you *quickly* convince the farmer that it would be much better to serve roast beef? On the back of this page or on a separate sheet of paper, list at least 20 delightfully convincing ideas.

Teaching Suggestions for
IMAGINE THAT!?

Creative-Thinking Objectives

Originality
Elaboration

Activity Introduction

1. Distribute duplicated copies of the activity page.
2. Read aloud the two sets of directions on the page.
3. Let the pupils work on the activity independently.

Sample Student Responses

(They will vary greatly.)

Follow-Up Activities

1. *Wall Display:* Collect the completed activity pages and display them in a line along a wall so that the students can see and enjoy one another's creatures.
2. *Creative Writing:* Have the students each choose their favorite creature and write an original story called "A Day in the Life of . . . ." The completed stories can be displayed on a bulletin board for all to enjoy.

Name _____

IMAGINE THAT

1. Nothing like it has ever been seen before! It is soft and cuddly and eats only bubble gum. Draw its picture and invent a name for this creature.

This creature is a _____

2. This imaginary creature is *very* weird! Its many arms and feet make it truly unique. Draw a picture of this creature, then create a name for it.

This creature is a _____

List the unusual things this creature can do:

_____   _____

_____   _____

_____   _____

List the unusual problems this creature has:

_____   _____

_____   _____

Teaching Suggestions for
A MAGICAL SUITCASE

Creative-Thinking Objectives

Fluency
Flexibility
Originality

Activity Introduction

1. Hand out duplicated copies of the activity page.
2. Read aloud the activity situation on the page.
3. To warm up, let students brainstorm aloud three or four possibilities.
4. Group students in pairs and let each pair of students work together to develop an exciting list of at least 20 unusual things that their magical suitcase can do.

Sample Student Responses

- It automatically dry cleans any clothes that are packed in it.
- A loud siren goes off if someone tries to steal it.
- Just push a little button and it will give advice on interesting things to see while staying in a town or city.

Follow-Up Activities

1. Distribute two pieces of paper (approx. 2" × 5") to each pair of students. Have each group select their two favorite ideas from their lists and neatly write each idea on a separate piece of paper. The students then attach their two ideas to a real suitcase using loops of masking tape. Display the suitcase so that students can read one another's ideas during free time.
2. *Demonstration Speeches:* Have volunteer pairs of students prepare and perform demonstration speeches showing what their magical suitcases can do. This activity can be enlivened with props and creative showmanship.

Name _____

Imagine that you have a most unusual magical suitcase! On the lines below begin listing at least 20 wild and wonderful things it can do. Number each idea and continue your ideas on the back of this page or on a separate sheet of paper.

_____
_____
_____
_____
_____
_____
_____
_____
_____
_____
_____
_____
_____

Teaching Suggestions for
HOW TO KEEP A LEPRECHAUN

Creative-Thinking Objectives

Fluency
Flexibility
Originality

Activity Introduction

1. Distribute duplicated copies of the activity page.
2. Read aloud the activity instructions on the page.
3. Divide the class into groups of two or three students each. Let each group work together to complete the activity.
4. When they have completed their lists of at least 14 ideas, ask each group to circle the numeral in front of each idea they think no other group would have thought of.

Sample Student Responses

- Keep him in a cage in my bedroom until he becomes attached to me.
- Trick him into promising not to run away. Then hold him to his promise.

Follow-Up Activities

1. Let the groups share aloud ideas from their papers.
2. *Creative Writing:* Have the students write highly imaginative stories about their difficulties in keeping a leprechaun. Ideas from the activity pages will fire their imaginations as they write their stories.

Name _____

You have just caught a leprechaun! How are you going to keep him from getting away? Use your imagination and think of at least 14 ideas. Begin writing your ideas below and continue on the back of this page or on a separate sheet of paper. Number each idea and provide as much detail as possible. Then circle the numbers of the ideas you think no one else in your class would have thought of!

_____

_____

_____

_____

_____

_____

_____

_____

_____

_____

_____

_____

_____

_____

Teaching Suggestions for
THE EMPTY CAGE MYSTERY

Creative-Thinking Objectives

Fluency (Activity Introduction—Step 3)
Flexibility (Activity Introduction—Step 3)
Originality
Elaboration

Activity Introduction

1. Hand out duplicated copies of the activity page.
2. Have a volunteer read aloud the activity instructions on the page.
3. Divide the class into a number of teams to brainstorm ideas of what might have been in the cage. Each group should list their ideas on paper. Encourage the pupils to let their imaginations churn up some interesting and unusual possibilities!
4. Allow the groups adequate time to develop interesting ideas.
5. Let groups volunteer to share ideas of what might have been in the cage.
6. Now the pupils are ready to refer back to their individual activity pages, decide what was in the cage, and write an interesting story including information answering the questions on their activity page.
7. Encourage pupils to proofread their stories to locate and correct any errors and to make sure that the stories make sense.

Sample Student Responses

What was in the cage?

- The only abominable snowman ever captured
- A pair of unicorns
- An invisible gorilla
- A young dinosaur

Follow-Up Activities

1. Have students volunteer to read their stories to the class.
2. *Class Book:* Collect the complete student stories and staple them together with a construction paper cover to form a class book. Give the book a title such as "THE EMPTY CAGE MYSTERY STORIES" and place the book in a good location for student reading during free time.

Name _____

The cage door is open! But what has escaped? And how did it get out? Where is it lurking now? Use the lines below to tell about this mystery. Use the back of this page if you need more room.

_____

_____

_____

_____

_____

_____

_____

_____

_____

_____

_____

_____

_____

_____

_____

_____

_____

Teaching Suggestions for
SUPER HOUSE OF THE FUTURE

Creative-Thinking Objectives

Fluency
Flexibility
Originality
Elaboration (Follow-Up Activity 2)

Activity Introduction

1. Hand out duplicated copies of the activity page.
2. Read aloud the activity instructions on the page.
3. Encourage the students to give serious thought to the activity, coming up with new ideas of a house of the future that is much different from houses today. Each idea should have specific practical reasons for its use.
4. Have the students complete the activity independently during class time.

Sample Student Responses

New, undreamed of conveniences:

- Automatic furniture-duster built right into each room
- Automatic bed-maker

Follow-Up Activities

1. Write each of the four categories on a different section of the chalkboard. Let the pupils volunteer to share ideas from their papers, one category at a time. Write each idea on the chalkboard under the appropriate category.
2. *Super House Illustration:* Have the students choose ideas either from the activity page or from Follow-Up Activity 1 and draw either a floor plan or an illustration of a Super House of the Future. Colored pencils, markers, or crayons will enliven the illustration, as well as the addition of as much detail as possible. The completed illustrations may be displayed on the wall or a bulletin board for all to enjoy.

Name _____

Super House of the Future

What would a house of the future be like? How would it be heated and cooled? What new, undreamed-of labor-saving conveniences would it have? Design your own Super House of the Future by writing your ideas below. Make sure to include the practical reason for each item's existence in your description. No idea is too wild or farfetched! Use the back of this page if you need more room.

MATERIALS FROM WHICH THE HOUSE IS CONSTRUCTED: _____
_____
_____
_____
_____

METHODS OF HEATING AND COOLING: _____
_____
_____
_____
_____

NEW, UNDREAMED-OF LABOR-SAVING CONVENIENCES: _____
_____
_____
_____
_____
_____
_____
_____
_____

OTHER NEW AND UNIQUE FEATURES: _____
_____
_____
_____
_____
_____
_____
_____
_____

Teaching Suggestions for
WHERE ARE HIS SPOTS?

Creative-Thinking Objectives

Fluency
Flexibility
Originality
Elaboration (Follow-Up Activity 2)

Activity Introduction

1. Distribute duplicated copies of the activity page.
2. Read aloud the activity instructions.
3. Have a volunteer read aloud the example given on the activity page.
4. To further stimulate imaginations, let the pupils brainstorm aloud together two or three additional tall tale ideas of what might have happened to the giraffe's spots.
5. Have the pupils complete the activity independently.

Sample Student Responses

(See student activity page.)

Follow-Up Activities

1. Let the pupils volunteer to share aloud favorite ideas from their papers.
2. *Creative Writing:* Have each student choose his or her favorite idea from the activity page and use it as the basis for an original tall tale telling how the giraffe lost its spots. The completed tall tales can be bound into a class book, read aloud, or displayed on a bulletin board.
3. Have the pupils brainstorm aloud together highly imaginative ideas of how an alligator with no teeth might have lost them. Again, no idea is too far-fetched. As the ideas are suggested, list them on the chalkboard.

Name _____

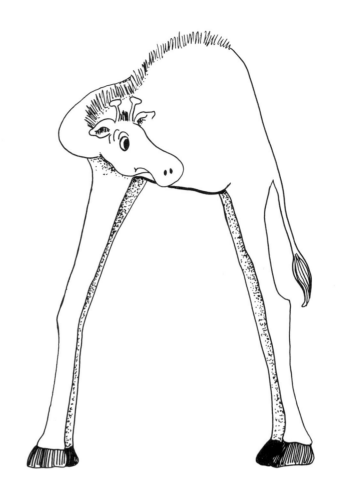

This giraffe has just discovered that he is missing his spots! What might have happened to them? List 14 highly imaginative ideas—no idea is too farfetched! One example is given below to get you started.

1. He had a bad sunburn and they all peeled off! _____

2. _____

3. _____

4. _____

5. _____

6. _____

7. _____

8. _____

9. _____

10. _____

11. _____

12. _____

13. _____

14. _____

15. _____

Teaching Suggestions for
DESIGN A CERTIFICATE OF AWARD

Creative-Thinking Objectives

Originality

Activity Introduction

1. Distribute duplicated copies of the activity page.
2. Read aloud the directions on the page.
3. Either make available or have students bring in sample certificates of award (for academic achievement, athletic achievement, outstanding attendance, and so on). Students should examine the awards to get a feeling for the type of wording found on awards and how they are laid out.
4. Have each student plan a sketch of his or her award on scrap paper and make a rough draft of the wording. Encourage the students to use imagination in designing the award using appropriate illustrations.
5. Point out to the students that the award does not have to be called a "Certificate of Award." It can be called anything their imaginations invent ("Certificate of Gluttony," "The Pizza Pig Award," and so on).
6. Students should make a final copy of the award on white art paper using whatever materials their cleverness suggests. Colored pencils, markers, crayons, and press-on lettering or designs would add strong appeal.

Sample Student Responses

(They will vary greatly.)

Follow-Up Activity

1. *Bulletin Board Display:* Collect the completed awards and display them on a bulletin board so that students can see and enjoy one another's ideas.

Name _____

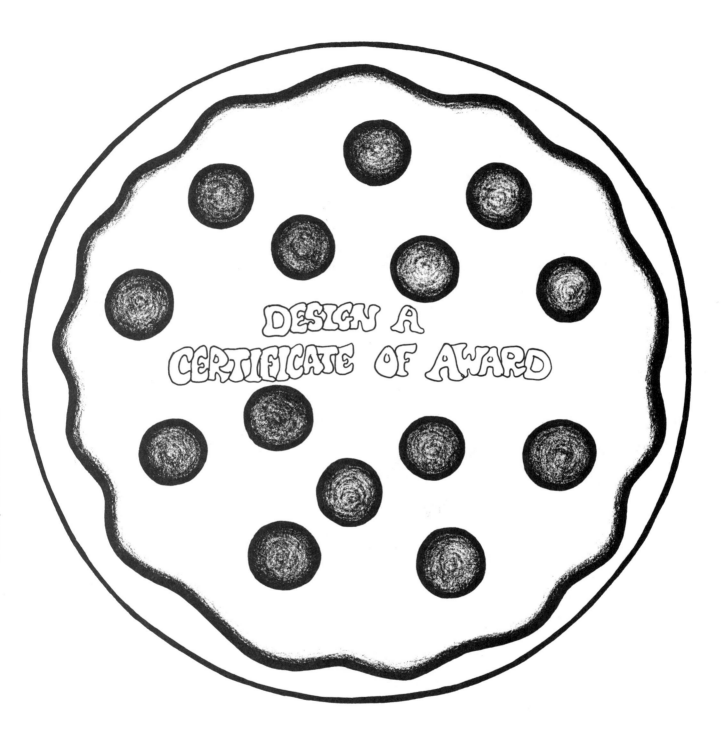

Your school will be conducting a Pizza-Eating Contest as a fund-raiser. You are in charge of designing the certificate of award for the winner! After you look at a few samples of actual awards, use your imagination to create a *really* original award. Be sure to include the wording on the certificate.

Teaching Suggestions for
INVENTIONS WANTED

Creative-Thinking Objectives

Originality
Elaboration

Activity Introduction

1. Hand out duplicated copies of the activity page.
2. Read aloud the activity instructions on the page.
3. Each pupil is to give careful thought to a new invention and complete his or her NEW INVENTION REGISTRATION FORM, including a neatly drawn and detailed diagram of the invention and an interesting and detailed description of the invention.
4. Allow sufficient time for pupils to complete the activity. Encourage pupils to carefully proofread their invention descriptions to catch and correct spelling, capitalization, and punctuation errors and to make sure it makes sense.

Sample Student Responses

- A flea-removing machine for use on pets
- A tornado repeller
- A youth-restoring machine

Follow-Up Activities

1. *Class Book:* Collect the completed activity pages and trim off the instructions at the top of each page with a paper cutter. Bind the "New Invention Registration Forms" together to form a NEW INVENTIONS CATALOG. Use two pieces of laminated construction paper for book covers and either staple the pages together or use more elaborate book-binding techniques such as yarn threaded through punched holes. Display the class book where it will be easily accessible for individuals to read during free time. An upper-level class may want to give its class book to a lower-level class for their enjoyment.

2. *Demonstration Speeches:* Have volunteers prepare and present demonstration speeches on their new inventions. Mock-ups of the inventions will enliven the presentations and a generous dash of humor will make them more fun for everyone.

Name _____

INVENTIONS WANTED

Ask yourself, "What do I wish I could have a machine do?" and then devise a new invention to do it! What will the invention look like? How will it operate? What will it be called? Use your powers of imagination to fill out the NEW INVENTION REGISTRATION FORM below. Continue on the back of this page if you need more room.

NEW INVENTION REGISTRATION FORM

Name of invention: _____

Name of inventor: _____

Diagram of invention:

Description of invention: _____
_____
_____
_____
_____
_____
_____
_____
_____
_____
_____
_____

Teaching Suggestions for
A PARROT WITH A BIG MOUTH!

Creative-Thinking Objectives

Fluency
Flexibility
Originality
Elaboration (Follow-Up Activity 2)

Activity Introduction

1. Distribute duplicated copies of the activity page.
2. Read aloud the instructions on the page.
3. Let the students read and laugh about the example.
4. Let the students brainstorm aloud a couple more ideas of things the parrot could have said that would have caused lots of trouble.
5. Let the students work on the activity independently during class time.

Sample Student Responses

(See student activity page.)

Follow-Up Activities

1. Let the students orally share favorite ideas with the rest of the class.
2. *Creative Writing:* Have each student choose his or her favorite idea from the activity page and develop it into a highly imaginative and humorous story about the problem caused by the big-mouthed parrot. The completed stories may be shared by volunteers reading aloud or through a bulletin board display.

Name _____

A Parrot with A Big Mouth!

Imagine you have a parrot that talks *too* much. And that parrot's big mouth has created some pretty big problems for you and your family!

Think of at least 14 different things that your parrot has said that have caused lots of trouble. One example is given here to get you started.

Begin writing your ideas on the lines below and continue on the back of this page or on a separate sheet of paper. Be sure to number each idea.

He told my Great-aunt Gertrude that I said she was

getting fat and should go on a diet!

_____

_____

_____

_____

_____

_____

_____

_____

_____

_____

_____

_____

Teaching Suggestions for
SELL A DINOSAUR EGG!

Creative-Thinking Objectives

Fluency
Flexibility
Originality
Elaboration

Activity Introduction

1. Distribute duplicated copies of the activity page.
2. Read aloud the instructions on the page.
3. To stimulate the flow of ideas, let the pupils brainstorm together ideas of what an amusement park could do with the dinosaur egg.
4. After many ideas have been suggested, let each pupil write the idea of his or her choice to complete item 1.
5. Follow the same procedure with item 2.
6. Then let the pupils complete the activity independently.

Sample Student Responses

- Sell it to a millionaire. He could hatch it and then give it to his children as the most unusual pet in the world!

Follow-Up Activities

1. Let pupils share ideas from their papers.
2. *Ad Writing:* Have each student choose his or her favorite idea and develop it into a magazine ad for the market chosen. Illustrations, photos cut from magazines, press-on lettering, and lots of color will contribute to an appealing ad. The complete ads can be displayed on a bulletin board for all to enjoy and chuckle over.

Name _____

SELL A DINOSAUR EGG!

Imagine that you have a real dinosaur egg that is about to hatch! You need to sell the egg, but whom could you sell it to and what could they do with it? Begin writing ten interesting and imaginative ideas below. Ideas 1 and 2 have been started for you. Continue writing your ideas on the back of this page or on a separate sheet of paper. Be sure to number each idea and provide as much detail as you can.

1.   I could sell it to an amusement park owner. He or she could . . .

_____

_____

2.   I could sell it to a witch. She could . . .

_____

_____

_____

_____

_____

_____

_____

_____

_____

Teaching Suggestions for
OH, FOR THE LIFE OF A FROG!

Creative-Thinking Objectives

Fluency
Flexibility

Activity Introduction

1. Distribute duplicated copies of the activity page.
2. Read aloud the instructions on the page.
3. Let the pupils work on the activity independently.

Sample Student Responses

- A frog can stay cool on a hot summer day.
- Frogs don't have to clean up their bedrooms!
- Frogs have an endless supply of bugs to eat!

Follow-Up Activities

1. Let pupils volunteer to share ideas from their papers.
2. *Mural:* Collect the completed student activity pages. Establish a committee of students to create an interesting and attractive mural proclaiming the advantages of the life of a frog. The committee can prepare the mural on a long piece of blue bulletin board paper (kraft paper) or on white butcher paper that has been fingerpainted with blue fingerpaint to produce a "watery" background. The committee can then select one or two ideas from each student paper to be used in the mural. The ideas can be written on green construction paper lily pads. The completed mural can be hung on the wall, providing students with an opportunity to read and enjoy one another's ideas.

Name _____

Imagine that you are a frog. What are ten advantages of your life style? List them on the lily pads and lines below. Then compare your answers with those of your classmates.

1. _____
_____
_____

2. _____
_____

3. _____
_____

OH, FOR THE LIFE OF A FROG!

5. _____
_____

6. _____
_____

4. _____
_____
_____

10. _____
_____
_____

7. _____
_____

8. _____
_____

9. _____

Teaching Suggestions for
PLEASE DON'T CUT ME DOWN!

Creative-Thinking Objectives

Fluency
Flexibility
Originality
Elaboration (Follow-Up Activity 2)

Activity Introduction

1. Distribute duplicated copies of the activity page.
2. Have a volunteer read the instructions on the page.
3. Let the pupils work on the activity independently.

Sample Student Responses

- I'd tell him that I was Abe Lincoln's favorite tree and that he simply can't cut me down for old Abe's sake.
- I'd tell him that the very last known pair of a rare species of bird has built a nest on one of my branches. If he chops me down he will be wiping out an endangered species!
- I'd tell him I was an explorer's landmark and I can't be cut down for historical reasons.

Follow-Up Activities

1. Let pupils volunteer to share ideas from their papers.
2. *Skits:* Divide the class into several groups and have each one prepare a skit of the encounter of the tree and the lumberjack. Ideas for the skits can come from the students' activity pages. The skits should include conversations between the tree and lumberjack, the tree's arguments, and the lumberjack's responses. The addition of simple costumes and a few props will add appeal.

PLEASE DON'T CUT ME DOWN!

If you were a tree about to be cut down by a lumberjack, how could you fast-talk your way out of your predicament? Think of at least 10 ideas and write them on the back of this page or on a separate sheet. Number each idea and provide as much detail as possible.

Teaching Suggestions for
WHILE WORKING IN MY LABORATORY
I CREATED A . . .

Creative-Thinking Objectives

Fluency
Flexibility
Originality
Elaboration (Follow-Up Activities 2 and 3)

Activity Introduction

1. Hand out duplicated copies of the activity page.
2. Read aloud the activity instructions.
3. Let the pupils complete the activity independently during class time. Encourage pupils to actually try to develop 22 ideas. Remember that the first ideas developed usually tend to be more commonplace. The more unusual and original ideas often are developed as the individual stretches his or her imagination to come up with more and more ideas.

Sample Student Responses

- A formula for increasing the thinking power of humans.
- A technique for changing teddy bears into cute little miniature-sized real bears.
- A fantastic new substance that is lightweight, stronger than steel, and absolutely indestructible for use in the manufacture of automobile bodies.

Follow-Up Activities

1. Let pupils volunteer to share ideas from their papers. Explain that they are to share only ideas different from those previously given. As ideas are shared, write them on the chalkboard.
2. *Illustrations:* Have each student choose a favorite idea from the activity page and draw a detailed picture or diagram of what was created. The completed illustrations can be hung as mobiles around the classroom or displayed on a bulletin board.
3. *Creative Writing:* Have each student select an interesting idea from the activity page and write a short story about how the thing was created and what happened afterward. The stories can be shared by volunteers reading aloud or displayed on a bulletin board.

Name _____

WHILE WORKING IN MY LABORATORY, I CREATED A...

Imagine that you're an exceptionally inventive research scientist.

List at least 22 of your wild and wonderful creations below. Nothing is too farfetched! Continue writing your ideas on the back of this page or on a separate sheet of paper and number each one.

_____
_____
_____
_____
_____
_____
_____
_____
_____
_____
_____
_____
_____
_____
_____

Teaching Suggestions for
THOUSANDS OF PUMPKINS!

Creative-Thinking Objectives

Fluency
Flexibility
Originality

Activity Introduction

1. Distribute duplicated copies of the activity page.
2. Read aloud the activity situation and problem on the page.
3. Let students work on the activity independently and provide sufficient class time for students to complete it.
4. Ask students to put a circle around the numeral in front of each idea they think no one else would have developed.

Sample Student Responses

Practical ways to get rid of the pumpkins:

- Give a free pumpkin to every school child in the community.
- Sell them to a company that cans pumpkin pie filling.

Follow-Up Activities

1. Let students volunteer to share aloud favorite practical ideas from their papers. Then let them share their favorite imaginative ideas.
2. *Pumpkin Illustrations:* Have each student draw a picture illustrating one of his or her ideas. A descriptive title for the picture should be included with it.

Name _____

Imagine that you are the Grand Winner of a contest and the prize is two truckloads of pumpkins! Two semi trucks have pulled up in front of your home and the drivers have unloaded the pumpkins in your front yard.

Your prize has been delivered! Now, how in the world are you going to get rid of that mountain of pumpkins? List below ten practical ideas and ten highly imaginative ideas for getting rid of the pumpkins.

Ten practical ways to get rid of the pumpkins:

1. _____
2. _____
3. _____
4. _____
5. _____
6. _____
7. _____
8. _____
9. _____
10. _____

Ten highly imaginative ways to get rid of the pumpkins:

1. _____
2. _____
3. _____
4. _____
5. _____
6. _____
7. _____
8. _____
9. _____
10. _____

Teaching Suggestions for
DON'T SLAY THE DRAGON!

Creative-Thinking Objectives

Fluency
Flexibility
Originality
Elaboration (Follow-Up Activity 2)

Activity Introduction

1. Distribute duplicated copies of the activity page.
2. Read aloud the activity instructions on the page.
3. To get ideas flowing, give the pupils several minutes to think of and write down one or two ideas.
4. Then let some pupils volunteer to read ideas from their papers.
5. Let the pupils complete the activity independently, developing ten new ideas different from those already shared aloud.

Sample Student Responses

- I may be the last dragon in existence! You wouldn't want to be responsible for the extinction of my species.
- If you don't kill me, I'll guard your castle and protect you from enemies.

Follow-Up Activities

1. Let students volunteer to share ideas from their papers.
2. *Creative Writing:* Ask each pupil to pretend to be the friendly dragon and write a persuasive newspaper editorial convincing the public that the knight should not be allowed to slay him or her. The pupils should use the reasons they developed on their activity papers when writing their editorials.

Name _____

DON'T SLAY THE DRAGON!

Pretend you are a friendly dragon.
List ten interesting and persuasive reasons why a brave knight
should not slay you!

1. _____
_____
2. _____
_____
3. _____
_____
4. _____
_____
5. _____
_____
6. _____
_____
7. _____
_____
8. _____
_____
9. _____
_____
10. _____
_____

REALISTIC CREATIVE-THINKING ACTIVITIES

Teaching Suggestions for
TRULY A MULTIPURPOSE ITEM

Creative-Thinking Objectives

Fluency
Flexibility
Originality
Elaboration (Follow-Up Activity 2)

Activity Introduction

1. Distribute duplicated copies of the activity page.
2. Read aloud the instructions on the page.
3. Let students work on the activity independently during class time.
4. Encourage the students to try to come up with 15 or more ideas. Remind them that the first ideas will probably come rather easily, but then will come more slowly. Ask them to keep stretching for more and more ideas even when the ideas start coming very slowly.

Sample Student Responses

- It could be used as a pretend hat by a three-year-old child.
- It could be used outside as a birdbath.

Follow-Up Activities

1. Let pupils volunteer to orally share ideas from their papers. As ideas are suggested, write them on the chalkboard.
2. *Demonstration Speech:* Have volunteers prepare and present their favorite ideas from the activity page as demonstration speeches. These should be done with a great deal of humor in the style of the TV ad for the product with "a million and one uses!" No props other than the mixing bowl should be used to encourage students to be creative and to pantomime.

Name _____

TRULY A MULTI-PURPOSE ITEM

Some objects can be used for many purposes other than their obvious and usual use. An unbreakable plastic mixing bowl is usually used for mixing ingredients when preparing food. However, with a little imagination, a plastic mixing bowl could be used for a wide variety of other purposes, both inside the house and outdoors!

List at least 20 unusual but useful ways to use an unbreakable plastic mixing bowl.

1. _____
2. _____
3. _____
4. _____
5. _____
6. _____
7. _____
8. _____
9. _____
10. _____
11. _____
12. _____
13. _____
14. _____
15. _____
16. _____
17. _____
18. _____
19. _____
20. _____

Teaching Suggestions for
HAPPY BIRTHDAY, MOM!

Creative-Thinking Objectives

Fluency
Flexibility
Originality

Activity Introduction

1. Pass out duplicated copies of the activity page.
2. Read aloud the activity situation on the page.
3. To stimulate the generation of ideas, let the students brainstorm aloud some ideas of possible presents.
4. After some interesting ideas have been presented, let the students begin writing down 20 of their own original ideas on their papers. As the students work on their lists of ideas, walk around the room pausing here and there to read ideas and to make appreciative comments.

Sample Student Responses

- Make a certificate promising to help her fold the clothes for one month.
- Go into the scrap material box and make four decorative potholders for her.
- Wash and wax her car for her.
- Serve her breakfast in bed.

Follow-Up Activities

1. Let students share aloud favorite ideas from their papers.
2. *Crafts:* Have each student actually make a no-cost gift for Mom using an idea from the activity sheet. The gift should have a practical use but consist of entirely free components. The gifts may also be given to Mom on Mother's Day.

Name _____

Happy Birthday, Mom!

Imagine that your mother's birthday is only two weeks away. You want to give her a birthday gift, but you are flat broke and have no way of earning money in time. What could you give to Mom? Think of at least 20 practical gifts for Mom that don't cost anything but that Mom would like. Write your ideas on the lines below and number each one. Continue writing ideas on the back of this page or on a separate sheet of paper. Provide as much detail as you can!

_____

_____

_____

_____

_____

_____

_____

_____

_____

_____

_____

Teaching Suggestions for
RAINDROPS KEEP FALLING!

Creative-Thinking Objective

Fluency

Activity Introduction

1. Hand out duplicated copies of the activity page.
2. Ask the students to develop a list of 18 really different things to do on a rainy afternoon. Have them include ways they can use their five senses and physical activity to have fun.

Sample Student Responses

- Food taste-testing
- Draw a map of my room
- Listen and name 20 different sounds in my room

Follow-Up Activities

1. Ask students to select the three ideas they like best on their papers. Have them lightly shade in with pencil or with blue crayon the three raindrops containing those three ideas.
2. Let students share aloud some of their favorite ideas from their papers.
3. *Bulletin Board Display:* Create a three-dimensional umbrella in the center of a bulletin board. Cut umbrella sections from different-colored pieces of construction paper and staple them to the board so they balloon out. Use a flat piece of construction paper for the handle. Have each student cut out a large raindrop of light blue construction paper. Then have them either write a favorite rainy-day activity in neat lettering on the raindrop or illustrate an activity and provide a caption. Give the bulletin board a title like "What to Do on a Rainy Day."

Name _____

RAINDROPS KEEP FALLING!

Inside each raindrop list something really different to do on a rainy day. These should be things you could really do.

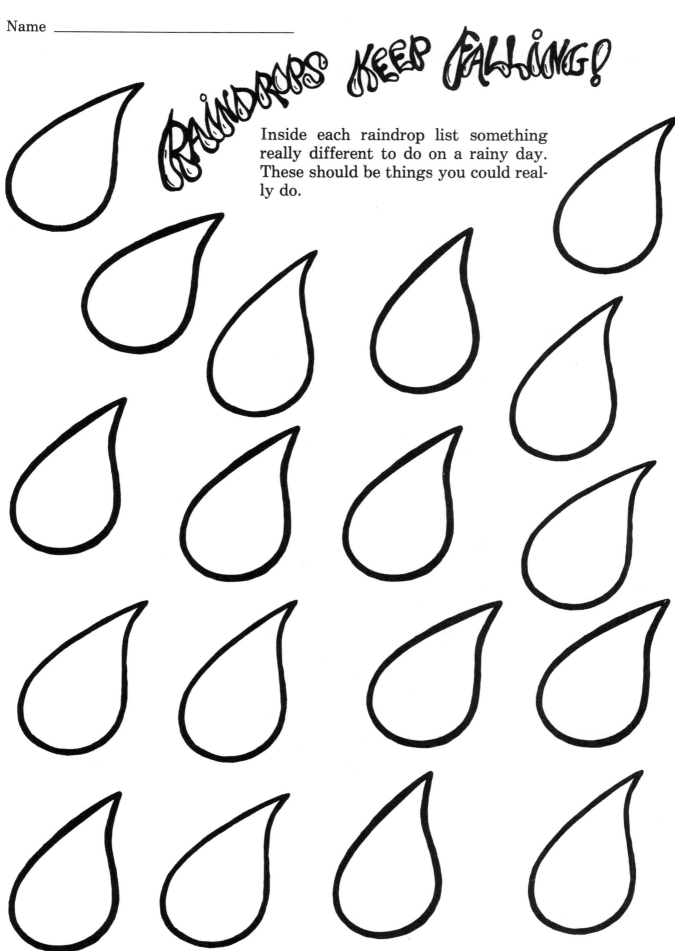

Teaching Suggestions for
A QUARTER SAVED . . .

Creative-Thinking Objectives

Fluency
Flexibility

Activity Introduction

1. Hand out duplicated copies of the activity page.
2. Read aloud the activity instructions on the page.
3. To warm up, give the group approximately two minutes to think of some possibilities. Then let volunteers share some ideas.
4. Group students in threes and let each group work together to develop a long list of ways to economize.
5. Remind groups that the ideas *must* be realistic!
6. Encourage each group to actually develop a list of at least 20 ideas.

Sample Student Responses

- Shut off lights in rooms not in use
- Write letters instead of making long-distance calls to relatives
- Set the thermostat two degrees lower in the winter

Follow-Up Activities

1. Let the various groups share some of their favorite ideas from their papers.
2. *Class Book:* Establish a student committee to develop an interesting and attractive booklet of suggestions for families who wish to economize. The committee should collect the groups' activity papers and select appropriate ideas for the booklet. Each idea may be illustrated with a caption noting the economical tip. The completed booklet may be duplicated by machine, assembled, and distributed for students to take home and use.

Name _____

A Quarter Saved...

How can you and your family save money around the house? List at least 20 practical ways for your family to economize.

1. _____
2. _____
3. _____
4. _____
5. _____
6. _____
7. _____
8. _____
9. _____
10. _____
11. _____
12. _____
13. _____
14. _____
15. _____
16. _____
17. _____
18. _____
19. _____
20. _____

Teaching Suggestions for
IN THE RESTAURANT BUSINESS

Creative-Thinking Objectives

Fluency
Flexibility
Originality

Activity Introduction

1. Distribute duplicated copies of the activity page.
2. Read aloud the activity instructions on the page.
3. Let students gather in groups of two or three and brainstorm together to develop their lists during class time. As students are working together, walk slowly among the groups, stopping occasionally to listen to an idea being discussed or to look at ideas written down thus far. Praise student ideas with positive comments, such as:

   "My, what a great idea!"
   "This group is developing a really excellent list!"
   "Good ideas! Keep them coming!"
   "Your ideas are very creative!"
   "I like the variety of ideas you are developing!"

Sample Student Responses

   Ideas for improving the restaurant:

- Hire more people to work behind the counter to speed up service.
- Make sure all employees are extrapolite and friendly to the customers.
- Hire three boys to be "carryout boys" to help people bring big orders to their cars.

Follow-Up Activities

1. Let student groups volunteer to share orally favorite ideas from their papers.
2. *TV Commercial Storyboard:* Have each student group develop a TV commercial for a fast-food restaurant using the ideas from the activity page. Each scene of the commercial should be sketched inside a TV tube-shaped box with the script for the scene and any audio effects (music, sounds, etc.) written below. Some groups may volunteer to actually perform the commercial for the class!

Name _____

IN THE RESTAURANT BUSINESS

You are the new owner of a fast-food restaurant! You want to improve it in the best ways possible to attract lots of customers. List eight ideas for improving the restaurant and eight ideas for attracting more customers below.

IDEAS FOR IMPROVING THE RESTAURANT:

1. _____
2. _____
3. _____
4. _____
5. _____
6. _____
7. _____
8. _____

IDEAS FOR ATTRACTING MORE CUSTOMERS:

1. _____
2. _____
3. _____
4. _____
5. _____
6. _____
7. _____
8. _____

Teaching Suggestions for
HOW CAN I THANK YOU?

Creative-Thinking Objectives

Fluency
Originality (Follow-Up Activity 2)
Elaboration (Follow-Up Activity 2)

Activity Introduction

1. Distribute duplicated copies of the activity page.
2. Read aloud the directions on the page.
3. Have the pupils work on the activity independently.

Sample Student Responses

(See student activity page.)

Follow-Up Activities

1. Let pupils volunteer to share ideas from their papers. Remind pupils that they should share aloud only those ideas that have not already been shared. As each idea is given, write it on the chalkboard for all to see.
2. *Creative Writing:* Have each student transform the activity page ideas into a rhyming or nonrhyming poem. Volunteers can share their poetry aloud.

Name _____

How Can I Thank You?

A friend has just given you a super present! How many ways can you think of to say thank you? Be as imaginative as you can. Two examples are given here.

1. __I appreciate your thoughtfulness!__ _____
2. __What a great gift! Thanks!__ _____
3. _____
4. _____
5. _____
6. _____
7. _____
8. _____
9. _____
10. _____

11. _____
12. _____
13. _____
14. _____
15. _____
16. _____
17. _____
18. _____
19. _____
20. _____

Teaching Suggestions for
NEW USES FOR EVERYDAY OBJECTS I

Creative-Thinking Objectives

Fluency
Flexibility
Originality

Activity Introduction

1. Distribute duplicated copies of the activity page.
2. Read aloud the activity instructions on the page.
3. To warm up, give the pupils two or three minutes to think of some different and unusual, but *practical*, uses for a toothbrush. Then let pupils volunteer to share some of those ideas orally.
4. Have the pupils complete the activity independently during class time.
5. Tell the pupils that when they have finished developing 12 different uses for each of the objects listed on the activity page, they are to think of other common objects and list uses for them.

Sample Student Responses

A soup spoon:

1. A spade for a large flowerpot
2. An ice cracker

Follow-Up Activities

1. Let pupils volunteer to share ideas from their papers, one category at a time.
2. Let the pupils share the ideas they developed of other objects that could be used in ways other than their normal use.
3. *Demonstration Speeches:* Have volunteers prepare and present demonstration speeches of the many uses for their favorite object. These should be humorous speeches in the style of the "handy, dandy" multipurpose implements advertised on TV.

Name _____

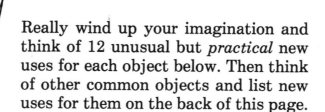

New Uses for Everyday Objects I

Really wind up your imagination and think of 12 unusual but *practical* new uses for each object below. Then think of other common objects and list new uses for them on the back of this page.

A SOUP SPOON:

1. _____
2. _____
3. _____
4. _____
5. _____
6. _____
7. _____
8. _____
9. _____
10. _____
11. _____
12. _____

A BRICK:

1. _____
2. _____
3. _____
4. _____
5. _____
6. _____
7. _____
8. _____
9. _____
10. _____
11. _____
12. _____

A FLOWERPOT:

1. _____
2. _____
3. _____
4. _____
5. _____
6. _____
7. _____
8. _____
9. _____
10. _____
11. _____
12. _____

A BLANKET:

1. _____
2. _____
3. _____
4. _____
5. _____
6. _____
7. _____
8. _____
9. _____
10. _____
11. _____
12. _____

Teaching Suggestions for
NAME THAT DOG

Creative-Thinking Objectives

Fluency
Originality
Elaboration (Follow-Up Activity 2)

Activity Introduction

1. Hand out duplicated copies of the activity page.
2. Read aloud the activity instructions on the page.
3. Open an encyclopedia to pictures of the various breeds of dogs so that any student unsure of the appearance of one of the breeds listed in the activity can look at a picture of it.
4. During class time, let the pupils work on the activity independently or group students in pairs and let each pair work together to develop names for the various puppies.

Sample Student Responses

Poodle name possibilities:

- Suzette
- Monsieur
- Francine

Follow-Up Activities

1. Write the names of the six breeds of dogs on the chalkboard. As the pupils or groups share aloud their favorite names for each type of puppy, one breed at a time, write the suggested names in a column under the appropriate breed name. Then let the class vote on the names to determine the class' favorite name for each type of puppy. The voting can be done by secret ballot one breed at a time.
2. *Creative Writing:* Have each student choose his or her favorite breed of dog and name and write an original story about getting the dog and naming it. The story can be written from the point of view of the student or the dog and should be written in the first person. Volunteers may read their stories aloud for the enjoyment of the whole class.

Name _____

Much thought should go into selecting a good name for a new puppy. The name should be interesting or appealing and should suit the characteristics of the breed of dog to be named. The new owner usually narrows name possibilities to three or four good ones, then selects the name that seems best.

Imagine that you are the new owner of each of the dogs below and you need to select a good name for each one! Carefully think of three or four names for each puppy, then circle the final name choice for each dog.

POODLE

_____

_____

_____

_____

GERMAN SHEPHERD

_____

_____

_____

_____

GOLDEN RETRIEVER

_____

_____

_____

_____

BEAGLE

_____

_____

_____

_____

BOXER

_____

_____

_____

GREAT DANE

_____

_____

_____

Teaching Suggestions for
MY BEST BACK YARD

Creative-Thinking Objectives

Fluency
Elaboration (Follow-Up Activities 2 and 3)

Activity Introduction

1. Hand out duplicated copies of the activity page.
2. Read aloud the activity instructions on the page.
3. Allow students adequate time to develop a list of 20 ideas for improving their yards. Encourage the pupils to actually develop at least 20 ideas. Students with more ideas can continue writing them on the back of the page.

Sample Student Responses

- Build an in-ground swimming pool in the back yard.
- Build a treehouse in the big maple tree in the back yard.

Follow-Up Activities

1. Let pupils volunteer to share favorite ideas from their papers.
2. *Map Making:* Have the students draw detailed maps of their back yards showing favorite ideas from the activity page. Illustrations of parts of the yard might accompany the map. A bulletin board display of the finished maps will allow the students to see one another's ideas.
3. *Yard Illustrations:* Have the students draw "before" and "after" illustrations of their yards. The ideas from the activity page should be incorporated in the "after" illustration. The finished drawings may be displayed on a bulletin board or wall.

Name _____

Think of your back yard at home. How could you make it the best back yard it could be? What changes could be made? What could be added or taken away? List at least 20 practical ideas. Remember, these must be things you could actually do to improve your yard! Number each idea and continue writing ideas on the back of this page or on a separate sheet of paper.

_____
_____
_____
_____
_____
_____
_____
_____
_____
_____
_____
_____

Teaching Suggestions for
FIRE: GOOD AND BAD

Creative-Thinking Objectives

Fluency
Flexibility

Activity Introduction

1. Distribute duplicated copies of the activity page.
2. Read aloud the instructions on the page.
3. Ask pupils to think beyond the obvious and include at least 18 interesting, clever, and unusual answers.
4. Ask pupils to put a circle around the number of each idea they think no one else in the class would have thought of.

Sample Student Responses

GOOD:

- It can provide protection against some wild animals.
- It could be used to attract rescuers to a wrecked airplane.

BAD:

- It attracts mosquitoes on a summer night.
- It can char marshmallows to an inedible state.

Follow-Up Activities

1. Let pupils volunteer to share ideas. Explain that you want them to skip over the very obvious answers and share the ideas they consider the most interesting, clever, and unusual.
2. *Bulletin Board Display:* Have the students individually brainstorm on paper the good and bad aspects of *water.* Divide a bulletin board in half with a simple drawing of a waterfall and entitle the left side "GOOD" and the right side "BAD." Each student should choose a favorite good aspect and a favorite bad aspect and neatly write each on a blue construction-paper water drop and sign his or her name to each one. Staple the drops to the appropriate sides of the board so that students can see one another's ideas.

Name _____

Fire: Good and Bad

Fire has both good and bad aspects. Think of at least 18 interesting, clever, and unusual ways in which fire is good and 18 ways it is bad. List your ideas below and use the back of this page if you need more room.

GOOD:

1. _____
2. _____
3. _____
4. _____
5. _____
6. _____
7. _____
8. _____
9. _____
10. _____
11. _____
12. _____
13. _____
14. _____
15. _____
16. _____
17. _____
18. _____

BAD:

1. _____
2. _____
3. _____
4. _____
5. _____
6. _____
7. _____
8. _____
9. _____
10. _____
11. _____
12. _____
13. _____
14. _____
15. _____
16. _____
17. _____
18. _____

Teaching Suggestions for
NAME THAT PRODUCT!

Creative-Thinking Objectives

Fluency
Originality
Elaboration (Follow-Up Activity 2)

Activity Introduction

1. Hand out duplicated copies of the activity page.
2. Read aloud the instructions on the page.
3. Group students in threes and let each group brainstorm together to develop their various new product names.
4. Allow class time for the student groups to develop their ideas. As students are working together, walk slowly among the groups, stopping occasionally to listen to an idea being discussed or to look at ideas written down. Reward student ideas with positive and appreciative comments.

Sample Student Responses

A highly comfortable new brand of shoes:

- AIR-WALK
- DAY'S COMFORT
- STEP-EASE

Follow-Up Activities

1. Let student groups volunteer to share some of their favorite product names from their papers.
2. *Ad Writing:* Have each student group develop an ad for their favorite activity-page product. The ad could take the form of a radio or TV commercial or a magazine or newspaper ad. For a commercial, have the students include the script, sound effects or music, and visual scenes (if any). For a print ad, have the students develop a layout with cutout magazine lettering, drawings, or magazine photos. Students should refer to similar ads as they plan their own. The ads may be shared through presentations for the class or on a bulletin board or wall display.

Name _____

Much careful thought goes into the name of a new product. The name, if well chosen, can really give a boost to sales.

Imagine you are the new product manager of the six new products below. You must think of a good marketable name for each one. Brainstorm several names. Circle the name you like best for each product.

A highly comfortable new brand of shoes:	A new toothpaste: _____
_____	_____
_____	_____
_____	_____
_____	_____
_____	_____
_____	_____
_____	_____
A new dog food: _____	A new candy bar: _____
_____	_____
_____	_____
_____	_____
_____	_____
_____	_____
_____	_____
A new fuel-efficient, economy car: _____	A new, supersleek, sports car: _____
_____	_____
_____	_____
_____	_____
_____	_____
_____	_____

Teaching Suggestions for
WHAT CAN I MAKE?

Creative-Thinking Objectives

Fluency
Flexibility
Elaboration (Follow-Up Activity 2)

Activity Introduction

1. Distribute duplicated copies of the activity page.
2. Read aloud the activity situation and instructions on the page.
3. Let the pupils work on the activity independently during class time.

Sample Student Responses

- I could make Barbie doll clothes for my little sister.
- I could make a bird feeder.
- I could make a leather knifeholder.
- I could make a slingshot.

Follow-Up Activities

1. Let the students volunteer their best ideas from the activity page. As ideas are given, write them on the chalkboard.
2. *Writing Directions:* Have each student choose his or her favorite idea from the activity page and write specific directions for making the item. The students should first make notes of the complete materials needed. Then the student writes assembly directions in chronological order. The notes are then rewritten into clearly worded, step-by-step directions. The directions may be accompanied by a diagram or illustration of the item. Students may wish to swap directions and read them to see if they are clear and easy to follow.

Name _____

WHAT CAN I MAKE?

Imagine that it is a cold, rainy afternoon and you have nothing to do. You go up to the attic and begin looking through some old trunks. You find scraps of felt, pieces of cloth in various colors and sizes, good-quality lumber from 3″ to 18″ long, and an assortment of nice-sized pieces of leather.

Your imagination begins to work as you excitedly think of the many terrific things you can make with these materials! List your ideas in detail on the back of this page or on a separate sheet of paper.

Teaching Suggestions for
UNFINISHED PICTURES I

Creative-Thinking Objectives

Flexibility

Activity Introduction

1. Distribute duplicated copies of the activity page.
2. Read aloud the instructions on the page.
3. Let pupils brainstorm together ideas for the first unfinished picture.
4. Then let pupils complete the activity independently.

Sample Student Responses

Unfinished Picture 1:

- Ribbon candy
- A stretched spring
- An inchworm

Follow-Up Activities

1. Draw the first unfinished picture on a section of chalkboard. Let pupils volunteer to go to the chalkboard and quickly draw their completed version of it. After a number of completed versions of the first unfinished picture have been given, follow the same procedure with each of the remaining pictures.
2. *Ink-Blot Pictures:* Let the pupils make ink-blot pictures using tempera paint or watercolor paint. After the pictures have dried, let each student develop a list of things his or her picture could be. The finished pictures with captions may be displayed on a bulletin board or wall for all to enjoy.

Unfinished Pictures I

Each box below contains some lines of an unfinished picture. What could these unfinished pictures be? Use your imagination! On the lines under each unfinished picture, list six things the picture could be if it were finished.

Then select one of the possibilities for each unfinished picture and add lines to complete each. Compare your solutions and your pictures with your friends.

1. _____ 4. _____
2. _____ 5. _____
3. _____ 6. _____

1. _____ 4. _____
2. _____ 5. _____
3. _____ 6. _____

1. _____ 4. _____
2. _____ 5. _____
3. _____ 6. _____

1. _____ 4. _____
2. _____ 5. _____
3. _____ 6. _____

1. _____ 4. _____
2. _____ 5. _____
3. _____ 6. _____

1. _____ 4. _____
2. _____ 5. _____
3. _____ 6. _____

Teaching Suggestions for
IT'S A GOOD PLACE!

Creative-Thinking Objectives

Fluency
Originality (Follow-Up Activities 2 and 3)
Elaboration (Follow-Up Activity 3)

Activity Introduction

1. Hand out duplicated copies of the activity page.
2. Read aloud the activity instructions on the pupil page.
3. To get ideas started, let volunteers suggest a couple of ideas of good things to tell a creature from outer space.
4. Then let the pupils work on the activity independently.
5. Encourage pupils to give serious thought to their responses and to develop *at least* 20 ideas.

Sample Student Responses

- We have beautiful forests filled with squirrels, raccoons, and bears.
- We have rivers and lakes in which to swim and fish.
- We have parents who love us and take care of us.
- We have books filled with great stories.

Follow-Up Activities

1. Let pupils volunteer to share ideas from their papers.
2. *Posters or Collages:* Have the pupils develop posters or collages proclaiming some of the good things about the planet Earth. The finished art can be displayed on the classroom walls or in a hallway.
3. *Skits:* Have groups of students write entertaining skits featuring some "Earth people" discovering a UFO and meeting a space creature. Let volunteers act out their skits for the enjoyment of the class.

Name _____

IT'S A GOOD PLACE!

If you met a creature from outer space, what good things could you tell it about the planet Earth? List at least 20 ideas below and use the back of this page if you need more room.

1. _____
2. _____
3. _____
4. _____
5. _____
6. _____
7. _____
8. _____
9. _____
10. _____
11. _____
12. _____
13. _____
14. _____
15. _____
16. _____
17. _____
18. _____
19. _____
20. _____

Teaching Suggestions for
WITHOUT ELECTRICITY

Creative-Thinking Objectives

Fluency
Elaboration

Activity Introduction

1. Distribute duplicated copies of the activity page.
2. Read aloud the activity questions on the page.
3. Let the students brainstorm together three or four problems that they would experience if they had no electricity for three days.
4. Then let the students complete the activity independently.

Sample Student Responses

- Some heating systems wouldn't work.
- The refrigerator wouldn't work.
- There would be no TV.

Follow-Up Activities

1. Allow pupils to share ideas from their activity papers, giving first the problem and then an innovative solution.
2. *No Electricity Illustrations:* Have each student fold a piece of white drawing paper in half, crease along the fold, then unfold the paper. Each student should select his or her favorite problem from the activity page and illustrate it on the left half of the paper. On the right half, the student should draw the solution to the problem. The finished illustrations may be displayed on a bulletin board or wall for the entire class to see.

Name _____

Imagine that the electricity went off in your entire area for three days in the middle of winter. What problems would you experience? Which of these problems could you solve, and how would you solve them? On this page write at least 12 problems and a practical solution for each. Use the back of this page if you need more room.

PROBLEMS

1. _____
_____
2. _____
_____
3. _____
_____
4. _____
_____
5. _____
_____
6. _____
_____
7. _____
_____
8. _____
_____
9. _____
_____
10. _____
_____
11. _____
_____
12. _____
_____

SOLUTIONS

1. _____
_____
2. _____
_____
3. _____
_____
4. _____
_____
5. _____
_____
6. _____
_____
7. _____
_____
8. _____
_____
9. _____
_____
10. _____
_____
11. _____
_____
12. _____
_____

Teaching Suggestions for
CHALLENGING ABBREVIATIONS

Creative-Thinking Objectives

Fluency
Flexibility
Originality

Activity Introduction

1. Distribute duplicated copies of the activity page.
2. Read aloud the activity instructions on the page.
3. Have pupils look at the example given.

> IMPORTANT: Before pupils begin thinking of their own abbreviation meanings, make sure they clearly understand that no crude, off-color, cruel, or insulting meanings will be tolerated.

4. Give the pupils a minute to think of and write down other interesting, humorous, or unusual meanings for the example abbreviation.
5. Let pupils volunteer to share their ideas for the example.
6. Have pupils complete the activity independently during class time.

Sample Student Responses

W.I.T.
- Western Interstate Trucking
- Wave in Triumph!
- Win It Team!
- Winter In Tallahassee

Follow-Up Activities

1. Let pupils volunteer to share ideas from their papers.
2. *Abbreviation Mobiles:* Divide the class into 12 committees to make mobiles for the various abbreviations. Each committee should be assigned one of the activity abbreviations. Each committee should then proceed to make an interesting and attractive mobile with selected student nonabbreviated versions of the abbreviations dangling from the abbreviation. Each committee should determine from the class activity papers which nonabbreviated versions of the abbreviations they wish to use in their mobile.

   Hang the completed mobiles where pupils can read and enjoy one another's ideas.

Name _____

Twelve newly invented abbreviations appear below. In fact, these abbreviations are so new it is up to you to decide what each abbreviation stands for! Use your imagination to come up with some interesting, humorous, or unusual meanings for each of these abbreviations. An example is provided for you.

Example: W.I.T.—Wednesday Is Terrific

1. F.P.O.A. _____

2. O.U.C.H. _____

3. S.M.A.S.H. _____

4. H.O.G. _____

5. G.L.T.A. _____

6. A.T.I. _____

7. O.M.M. _____

8. B.F.A. _____

9. W.O.W. _____

10. H.I. _____

11. U.N.T.A. _____

12. C.D.A. _____

Teaching Suggestions for
BARRELS OF IDEAS!

Creative-Thinking Objectives

Fluency
Flexibility
Originality
Elaboration (Follow-Up Activity 2)

Activity Introduction

1. Distribute duplicated copies of the activity page.

2. Have a volunteer read aloud the activity instructions.

3. Point out to the pupils that the barrels could be sawed in half or in quarters, the bottom could be sawed off, or other modifications could be made.

4. To warm up, let the pupils brainstorm together two or three ideas of *decorative* things that could be made from a wooden barrel, and then two or three practical things that could be made from a barrel.

5. Ask the pupils to try to develop a list of at least 30 ideas, 15 decorative and 15 practical. Remind the pupils that the first ideas will come fairly easily. Then ideas will come more slowly. But point out to the pupils that you want them to continue working on developing more and more ideas even when the ideas start coming more slowly. Provide class time for the pupils to develop and write their ideas.

Sample Student Responses

- A toy box
- A lamp base
- A decorative fountain
- A bird beeder

Follow-Up Activities

1. Let pupils share orally ideas from their papers. As ideas are given, write them on the chalkboard.

2. *Writing Directions:* Have each student choose his or her favorite idea from the activity page and write directions for constructing it. First, a complete list of necessary materials should be given. Then clear, step-by-step directions should be developed.

Name _____

Barrels of Ideas!

How many interesting and useful things can be made from a wooden barrel? The barrel could be cut in any number of ways for different effects!

List at least 15 decorative ideas and 15 practical ideas for things made from barrels. Use the back of this page if you need more room.

DECORATIVE IDEAS	PRACTICAL IDEAS
1. _____	1. _____
2. _____	2. _____
3. _____	3. _____
4. _____	4. _____
5. _____	5. _____
6. _____	6. _____
7. _____	7. _____
8. _____	8. _____
9. _____	9. _____
10. _____	10. _____
11. _____	11. _____
12. _____	12. _____
13. _____	13. _____
14. _____	14. _____
15. _____	15. _____

Teaching Suggestions for
A BABYSITTER'S GUIDE

Creative-Thinking Objectives

Fluency
Flexibility
Originality

Activity Introduction

1. Distribute duplicated copies of the activity page.
2. Read aloud the activity instructions on the page.
3. Let the pupils work on the activity independently during class time.

Sample Student Responses

- Read stories to the child.
- Let the child help you fix lunch.
- Take the child on a "nature hike" in the back yard.

Follow-Up Activities

1. Let pupils volunteer to share ideas from their papers.
2. *Class Book:* Establish a committee of students to develop a "Babysitter's Guide" based on the ideas generated on the activity pages. The committee should collect the activity pages from the class and select appropriate ideas for the guidebook. The addition of illustrations or photos plus attractive type will give the book an appealing and interesting format. The completed guidebook may be placed in the classroom library or school library for student use, or it may be duplicated and copies made available to those students who are interested.

Name _____

A BABYSITTER'S GUIDE

You have a babysitting job with a four-year-old child for an entire day. List at least 18 good ways to keep the child occupied. Use wisdom and good judgement in developing your list, and remember that you must be able to carry out the ideas.

1. _____
2. _____
3. _____
4. _____
5. _____
6. _____
7. _____
8. _____
9. _____
10. _____
11. _____
12. _____
13. _____
14. _____
15. _____
16. _____
17. _____
18. _____

Teaching Suggestions for
UNFINISHED PICTURES II

Creative-Thinking Objective

Flexibility

Activity Introduction

1. Distribute duplicated copies of the activity page.
2. Read aloud the instructions on the page.
3. Let pupils brainstorm together ideas for the first unfinished picture.
4. Then let pupils complete the activity independently.

Sample Student Responses

Unfinished Picture 1:

- A candy cane's stripes
- The side of a roof
- A divided highway

Follow-Up Activities

1. Let students share ideas for each unfinished picture, one picture at a time. Write each idea on the chalkboard as it is given. If an idea is given that is difficult to visualize, a member of the class can ask that the pupil suggesting the idea go to the chalkboard and demonstrate the idea by quickly completing the unfinished picture.
2. *More Unfinished Pictures:* Have the students each develop a few unfinished pictures and then exchange and solve them.

Name _____

Unfinished Pictures II

Each box below contains some lines of an unfinished picture. What could these unfinished pictures be? Use your imagination! On the lines under each unfinished picture, list six things the picture could be if it were finished.

Then select one of the possibilities for each unfinished picture and add lines to complete each. Compare your solutions and your pictures with your friends.

1.

1. _____ 4. _____
2. _____ 5. _____
3. _____ 6. _____

2.

1. _____ 4. _____
2. _____ 5. _____
3. _____ 6. _____

3.

1. _____ 4. _____
2. _____ 5. _____
3. _____ 6. _____

4.

1. _____ 4. _____
2. _____ 5. _____
3. _____ 6. _____

5.

1. _____ 4. _____
2. _____ 5. _____
3. _____ 6. _____

6.

1. _____ 4. _____
2. _____ 5. _____
3. _____ 6. _____

Teaching Suggestions for
IDEAS FOR THE INVENTORS

Creative-Thinking Objectives

Fluency
Flexibility
Originality
Elaboration (Follow-Up Activities 2 and 3)

Activity Introduction

1. Distribute duplicated copies of the activity page.
2. Read aloud the activity instructions on the page.
3. Provide class time for the pupils to complete the activity independently.

Sample Student Responses

Inventions for the car:

- An instrument that prevents drunk drivers from being able to start the car
- A remote-control, radar device that senses when two or more vehicles are about to collide and triggers a strong, magnetic-repelling device to prevent the vehicles from actually crashing into each other

Follow-Up Activities

1. Let pupils volunteer to share favorite ideas from their papers, one category at a time.
2. *Ad Writing:* Have each pupil select a favorite invention idea from his or her activity page and create an advertisement for the fantastic new machine. The ad could incorporate drawings, photos cut from magazines, cutout type or press-on lettering, and the student's original copy. The finished ads may be displayed on a bulletin board or classroom wall.
3. *Descriptive Writing:* Have each student choose a favorite invention idea and write a detailed explanation of how the invention works.

Name _____

At one time or another we have all wished that someone would invent something to meet a particular need. Here is an opportunity to give some creative thought to some inventions that need to be invented. In each area below, describe one or more inventions that could actually be developed. Provide as much detail as possible. Use the back of this page if you need more room.

INVENTIONS FOR THE CAR:
_____
_____
_____
_____
_____
_____
_____
_____
_____
_____
_____
_____

INVENTIONS FOR HOME:
_____
_____
_____
_____
_____
_____
_____
_____
_____
_____
_____
_____

INVENTIONS FOR SCHOOL:
_____
_____
_____
_____
_____
_____
_____
_____
_____
_____
_____
_____

INVENTIONS FOR _____
_____
_____
_____
_____
_____
_____
_____
_____
_____
_____
_____
_____

Teaching Suggestions for
LET'S IMPROVE TV

Creative-Thinking Objectives

Fluency
Flexibility
Elaboration (Follow-Up Activity 2)

Activity Introduction

1. Distribute duplicated copies of the activity page.
2. Read aloud the activity instructions on the page.
3. To get ideas flowing, give pupils a couple of minutes to think of and write down one or two ideas.
4. Then let several pupils volunteer to read ideas from their papers.
5. Let the pupils complete the activity independently during class time, developing many more new ideas.

Sample Student Responses

- Have fewer commercials!
- Have more news about *good* things on the nightly news programs.

Follow-Up Activities

1. Let students volunteer to share favorite ideas from their papers.
2. *Editorial Writing:* Using the ideas from their activity pages, have the pupils write newspaper editorials suggesting ways that a television network could improve its programming and thus expand its popularity. The students should prepare a logical and persuasive statement of their ideas. They may want to look at some real editorials as models before they begin writing their own.

Name _____

Here's your opportunity to give your opinions about what a TV network should do to improve their programming and please their viewers! On the back of this page or on a separate sheet of paper, write at least ten ideas. Include as much detail as possible and keep the ideas practical.

Teaching Suggestions for
TRULY BEAUTIFUL THINGS!

Creative-Thinking Objectives

Fluency
Flexibility
Elaboration (Follow-Up Activity 2)

Activity Introduction

1. Distribute duplicated copies of the activity page.
2. Read aloud the activity instructions on the page.
3. Call on a volunteer to read the two examples.
4. Point out that the examples went beyond just saying "a waterfall" or "rain." Additional description was given to add interest and to help others picture in their minds the actual beauty of the scene. Also talk about how "beauty is in the eye of the beholder."
5. Ask the students to add enough interesting detail to each of their ideas to make the description very specific and real for the reader.

Sample Student Responses

Beautiful Things to See:
- A heavy snow making everything look like a picture on a Christmas card
- A mother deer and her fawn, graceful and alert, standing at the water's edge
- A cozy fire flickering peacefully in a fireplace

Beautiful Things to Hear:
- Birds singing on a beautiful spring morning
- The crowd cheering when you make the basket that wins the game
- Silence

Follow-Up Activities

1. Let students volunteer to share their ideas of beautiful things to see. Then let pupils share ideas of beautiful things to hear.
2. *Creative Writing:* Have each pupil select an idea of a beautiful thing from the activity page and write a poem about it or write a more elaborate description of it.
3. *Beautiful Things to Smell:* As an oral follow-up activity, let the pupils suggest beautiful things to *smell*. Write each idea on the chalkboard as it is suggested.

Name _____

Truly Beautiful Things!

List some things you think are truly beautiful to see and to hear. Make sure to include some interesting detail in your description to make the scene "come alive."

List 9 more beautiful things to see:

1. A waterfall in a wilderness. _____
2. _____
3. _____
4. _____
5. _____
6. _____
7. _____
8. _____
9. _____
10. _____

List 9 more beautiful things to hear:

1. Rain on the window when you're cozy inside your home. _____
2. _____
3. _____
4. _____
5. _____
6. _____
7. _____
8. _____
9. _____
10. _____

Teaching Suggestions for
A DOZEN SUPER TITLES FOR UNWRITTEN STORIES

Creative-Thinking Objectives

Fluency
Flexibility

Activity Introduction

1. Distribute duplicated copies of the activity page.
2. Read aloud the activity instructions on the page.
3. Let pupils work on the activity independently during class time.

Sample Student Responses

(They will vary widely.)

Follow-Up Activities

1. Let students volunteer to share favorite story titles from their papers.
2. *Story-Starter Murals:* Divide the class into large groups and give each one a long piece of kraft paper or butcher paper. Each group is to create a mural using selected story titles from their activity pages along with illustrative drawings or photos cut from magazines. The students could use appropriate lettering for each title; for example, a mystery title could be written in wiggly, spooky letters. The completed murals can be hung around the classroom as a rich source of story-starter ideas for creative-writing activities. Or, the murals could be hung up one at a time, displayed for a week or so, and used in creative-writing activities. In this way students would be provided with fresh story-starter ideas over an extended period of time.
3. *Story-Starter Idea File:* Collect the activity pages and file them for ready reference when planning creative-writing activities. Here's a wealth of creative-writing story starters!

Name _____

A DOZEN SUPER TITLES FOR UNWRITTEN STORIES

Think of 12 exciting, interesting, or highly intriguing titles for stories you might want to write someday. These could be animal stories, science fiction, mysteries, high-adventure stories, fairy tales, legends, tall tales, and so on.

From your ideas, select only the very best titles to write on the lines below.

1. _____

2. _____

3. _____

4. _____

5. _____

6. _____

7. _____

8. _____

9. _____

10. _____

11. _____

12. _____

Teaching Suggestions for
PLEASE BUY ME A RACCOON!

Creative-Thinking Objectives

Fluency
Flexibility
Originality
Elaboration (Follow-Up Activity 2)

Activity Introduction

1. Hand out duplicated copies of the activity page.
2. Read aloud the activity situation on the page.
3. To warm up, let the students brainstorm aloud a couple of ideas.
4. Let the pupils work on the activity independently during class time. Encourage them to develop a list of at least 15 ideas.

Sample Student Responses

- I'll go to the library and get a book on how to take care of raccoons and impress my parents with my knowledge of them.
- I'll promise I will take care of it. They won't ever have to feed it for me.
- I'll tell them that every kid needs a pet and this is the one I've always dreamed of having.
- I'll promise that I won't ask for another thing between now and Christmas if they'll just buy that raccoon for me.

Follow-Up Activities

1. Let students share ideas from their papers.
2. *Letter Writing:* Using the ideas from the activity page, have each student write a persuasive letter to his or her parents to convince them to buy the raccoon for the student.

Name _____

PLEASE BUY ME A RACCOON!

You have always wanted a raccoon for a pet. The pet store has never had one for sale before, but now it does! Your parents are *far* from enthusiastic about buying a raccoon for a pet. On the back of this page or on a separate sheet of paper, write at least 15 ideas to convince them!

Teaching Suggestions for
TWENTY QUESTIONS ON THE U.S.A.

Creative-Thinking Objectives

Fluency
Flexibility
Originality

Activity Introduction

1. Hand out duplicated copies of the activity page.
2. Have a volunteer read the activity instructions and the sample question on the page.
3. Ask pupils to think of and write 20 more questions for which the answer could be *The United States.*
4. Let the pupils work in groups of three to develop their lists of questions. As the groups are completing their lists, ask them to look back over their lists and circle questions they think no other group would have developed.

Sample Student Responses

- What country has the bald eagle as its symbol?
- Uncle Sam stands for what country?
- What country borders Canada to the south?

Follow-Up Activities

1. Let the groups share some of their best questions from their papers. Explain that they are to share only questions different from those previously given.
2. *Bulletin Board Display:* Create a "The Answer Is: (name of your school)" bulletin board to which the students contribute appropriate questions. In the center of the board you could have a drawing of the school done by you, a volunteer student, or a group of students. Provide plenty of tacks or have a stapler near the board so that students can post their contributions written neatly on 4" × 6" pieces of paper.

Name _____

What country elects a president once every four years? The answer is: The United States. On the lines below write 19 more questions answerable by "The United States."

1. What country elects a president once every four years?   The U.S.A. ____
2. _____
3. _____
4. _____
5. _____
6. _____
7. _____
8. _____
9. _____
10. _____
11. _____
12. _____
13. _____
14. _____
15. _____
16. _____
17. _____
18. _____
19. _____
20. _____

Teaching Suggestions for
WHAT WILL YOU DO
IN THE WILDERNESS?

Creative-Thinking Objectives

Fluency
Flexibility
Originality
Elaboration

Activity Introduction

1. Distribute duplicated copies of the activity page.
2. Read aloud the activity situation on the page.
3. Let the pupils work on the activity independently during class time.

Sample Student Responses

- I would follow the deer trails and quietly learn all I could about the habits of the deer.
- I would make a collection of interesting and unusual stones.
- I would explore the mountain streams.
- I would go fishing early each morning and fry my fish on the shore.

Follow-Up Activities

1. Have students volunteer to share some of their favorite ideas from their papers.
2. *Creative Writing:* Have each student choose one of his or her ideas and use it as the basis for an original story or a detailed description. The idea might concern an adventure he would have, something she would explore, something he would make, or something she would do. The finished pieces could be displayed on a bulletin board.

WHAT WILL YOU DO IN THE WILDERNESS?

You are spending a month with a distant relative in a mountain cabin surrounded by a dense forest. You are miles from the nearest town and have no TV. The cottage is well supplied with an exciting variety of materials, tools, and equipment; there are beautiful lakes and streams nearby and interesting wildlife in the forest.

How will you occupy yourself for the entire month? What adventures will you have? What will you make? What will you explore? What experiments will you perform? On the back of this page or on a separate sheet of paper, list at least 12 detailed ideas.

Teaching Suggestions for
RAIN: GOOD AND BAD

Creative-Thinking Objectives

Fluency
Flexibility
Originality

Activity Introduction

1. Distribute duplicated copies of the activity page.
2. Read aloud the instructions on the page.
3. Ask the pupils to continue thinking beyond the obvious answers and include many interesting, clever, colorful, creative, and unusual answers.
4. Ask the pupils to put a circle around the numeral in front of each idea that they think no one else in the class would have thought of.

Sample Student Responses

Good:

• It settles the dust on dusty roads.
• It provides the relaxing sound of raindrops on the roof.

Bad:

• You can't get a suntan in the rain!
• It makes people carry umbrellas.

Follow-Up Activities

1. Let students volunteer to share ideas. Explain that you want them to skip over the very obvious answers and share the ideas they consider the most interesting, clever, creative, and unusual—the ones that perhaps no one else would have thought of.
2. *Creative Writing:* Have each student use his or her ideas as the basis for a poem about rain. The poem might include only the good aspects, the bad aspects, or both aspects of rain. It could be a rhyming or blank-verse poem, and could be humorous or serious. The completed poetry can be shared through volunteer readings or through a bulletin board display.

Name _____

Rain has both good and bad aspects. Think of at least 18 interesting, clever, and unusual ways in which rain is good, and 18 ways it is bad. List your ideas below and use the back of this page if you need more room.

GOOD:

1. _____
2. _____
3. _____
4. _____
5. _____
6. _____
7. _____
8. _____
9. _____
10. _____
11. _____
12. _____
13. _____
14. _____
15. _____
16. _____
17. _____
18. _____

BAD:

1. _____
2. _____
3. _____
4. _____
5. _____
6. _____
7. _____
8. _____
9. _____
10. _____
11. _____
12. _____
13. _____
14. _____
15. _____
16. _____
17. _____
18. _____

Teaching Suggestions for
MY PERFECT BEDROOM

Creative-Thinking Objectives

Fluency
Elaboration (Follow-Up Activity 3)

Activity Introduction

1. Distribute duplicated copies of the activity page.
2. Read aloud the activity instructions on the page.
3. Tell the pupils to be sure to include interesting and informative detail with each idea. For example, instead of saying "New carpet," they should include a more detailed description of what they have in mind, such as " A plush, royal blue, wall-to-wall carpet."
4. Provide ample class time for pupils to list at least 20 ideas.

Sample Student Responses

- Rich, warm-looking wood paneling for the walls
- A built-in wall-to-ceiling bookcase along one wall

Follow-Up Activities

1. *Bulletin Board Displays:* Display the completed activity pages on a bulletin board so that students can read and enjoy one another's ideas.
2. *The Perfect Classroom:* Have the students list ways to make their classroom perfect. The ideas do not need to be financially realistic.
3. *Perfect Bedroom Illustrations:* Have each student draw a picture of his or her perfect bedroom. Color can be added with paint or other media, and fabric swatches and paint chips can be glued alongside the drawing just as an interior decorator would do to show placement.

Name _____

MY PERFECT BEDROOM

To make your bedroom absolutely perfect, how would you change it? On the back of this page or on a separate sheet of paper, list at least 20 detailed ideas.

POTATO CHIPS

Teaching Suggestions for
PLAY WITH WORDS!

Creative-Thinking Objectives

Fluency

Activity Introduction

1. Distribute duplicated copies of the activity page.
2. Read aloud the activity instructions on the page.
3. Tell pupils that this will be a contest to see who can think of the most words!
4. Allow sufficient time for pupils to develop long lists of words.

Sample Student Responses

PLOW	HIT	DOT	SOW	SAW
LAY	PLY	ROT	LOW	PAW
IT	SIT	LOT	WOW	RAW
WIT	OAT	HOT	TOW	LAW
SWORD	POT	ROW	DRAW	TRAY

Follow-Up Activities

1. Determine which pupil has listed the most words. Look over that pupil's list to make sure that the words have not been repeated and that all words are appropriate according to the instructions on the pupil page. The pupil with the most words is then declared the contest winner.

2. *Bulletin Board Display:* Designate a section of a bulletin board for a class word game. Have a student volunteer cut large, colorful construction paper letters spelling "WHAT CAN YOU SPELL?" and staple them near the top of the board. For a one- or two-week period ask the students to contribute new words made only from the letters in the bulletin board title. Each letter may be used any number of times, but the *s* may not be added to make the plural of a word already contributed. The new words should be neatly written on 3″ × 2″ pieces of paper and a stapler located near the board so students can post their own answers. At the end of the time period, go over the list with the whole class. If you wish, use another phrase and replay the game!

Name _____

See how many words you can make using only the letters in the words PLAY WITH WORDS! Use each letter any number of times, but do not simply add the *s* to a word already listed to make another word. Write your words on the lines below and use the back of this page if you need more room.

Teaching Suggestions for
TWENTY QUESTIONS ON GLUE

Creative-Thinking Objectives

Fluency

Activity Introduction

1. Hand out duplicated copies of the activity page.
2. Have a volunteer read the activity instructions on the page.
3. Ask pupils to develop lists of twenty or more questions for which the answer could be *glue*.
4. Let the pupils work in pairs during class time to develop their lists of questions. As the pairs of students are completing their lists, ask them to look back over their lists and circle questions they think no other group would have developed.

Sample Student Responses

- What is a great "fix-it" item?   glue
- What can be used for art projects?   glue

Follow-Up Activities

1. Let the pairs volunteer to share some of their best questions from their papers. Explain that they are to share *only* questions different from those previously given.
2. *More "Twenty Questions"*: Have each student independently write a "Twenty Questions" subject at the top of a sheet of paper. Students then exchange papers and complete one another's papers. The finished papers may be shared aloud or through a bulletin board display.

Name _____

TWENTY QUESTIONS ON GLUE

What shouldn't you pour on your hair? The answer is: glue! Think of 20 more questions for which the answer is *glue*. Write your ideas below.

1. _____
2. _____
3. _____
4. _____
5. _____
6. _____
7. _____
8. _____
9. _____
10. _____
11. _____
12. _____
13. _____
14. _____
15. _____
16. _____
17. _____
18. _____
19. _____
20. _____

Teaching Suggestions for
DESIGN A WORD-SEARCH PUZZLE!

Creative-Thinking Objectives

Fluency

Activity Introduction

1. Distribute duplicated copies of the activity page.
2. Read aloud the directions on the page.
3. Have some samples of published "word-find" or "word-search" puzzles for the pupils to examine.
4. Encourage the students to develop their puzzles using only words from a specific subject or category of their choice (such as Christmas words, zoo animals, names of flowers, states in the United States, rivers of the world, and so on).
5. Have dictionaries readily available for student reference so that all words in the student puzzles will be spelled correctly.
6. Have a set of encyclopedias ready as a resource for developing word lists in some topic areas.
7. Have each pupil begin by deciding on the category of words he or she will use in the puzzle. Then have the pupils list related words on scratch paper. After many possible words have been listed and the accuracy of spelling has been checked, the pupils should begin working the words into the puzzle.

Sample Student Responses

(They will vary greatly.)

Follow-Up Activities

1. *Class Puzzle Challenges:* Occasionally duplicate one of the students' word-search puzzles for the entire class to work on during free time.
2. *More Word-Search Puzzles:* Have graph paper available for students who wish to create more word-search puzzles. At the same location provide a place for students to make their finished puzzles available for other students to work on.

DESIGN A WORD SEARCH PUZZLE!

Category: _____

You have been hired by the publisher of "Word-Search Puzzle Magazine" to devise an original puzzle.

First examine a few published word-search puzzles to get the feel for how to write one. Then think of a word category for your puzzle and write it above the grid.

Develop your puzzle using a pencil and write the words on scratch paper. When you are pleased with the puzzle, darken the letters with pen and write the Word List in alphabetical order at the bottom half of this page.

Have a friend try your puzzle!

© 1985 by The Center for Applied Research in Education, Inc.

Name _____

WORD-SEARCH PUZZLE WORD LIST:

Teaching Suggestions for
HOW THE WINDOW GOT BROKEN

Creative-Thinking Objectives

Fluency
Flexibility
Originality
Elaboration (Follow-Up Activity 2)

Activity Introduction

1. Distribute duplicated copies of the activity page.
2. Read aloud the activity instructions on the page.
3. Have a volunteer read aloud the example given on the activity page.
4. Point out to the students that the ideas they develop should be realistic possibilities even if they are highly unlikely!
5. To further stimulate imaginations, let the students brainstorm aloud together two or three additional ideas of how that window might have been broken.
6. Then let the pupils complete the activity independently during class time.

Sample Student Response

(See student activity page.)

Follow-Up Activities

1. Let the pupils volunteer to share aloud favorite ideas from their papers.
2. *Creative Writing:* Have each student write a tall tale describing how the window was broken. Emphasize that the tale should be humorous and need not be realistic. The finished tall tales may be shared aloud or displayed on a bulletin board or wall.

Name _____

How the Window Got Broken

One of the windows in your school has been broken. No one is sure how it happened. How do *you* think it got broken? On the lines below begin writing 20 realistic but very interesting ideas. Continue writing your ideas on the back of this page or on a separate sheet of paper.

1. A hungry hawk saw the hamster in a cage through the window, and flew right into the window to get it! _____

2. _____
    _____

3. _____
    _____

Teaching Suggestions for
USE THOSE CHRISTMAS CARDS!

Creative-Thinking Objectives

Fluency
Flexibility
Originality

Activity Introduction

1. Distribute duplicated copies of the activity page.
2. Read aloud the activity question on the page.
3. Point out to the students that some of their ideas might include uses of the cards in craft projects, uses of the cards with younger children, decorative uses of the cards, and so on.
4. Let the students work independently or in groups of two or three to develop ideas of uses for old Christmas cards.
5. Encourage the students to develop as many ideas as possible, writing additional ideas on another sheet of paper.

Sample Student Responses

- Glue them on an old wastebasket, then brush shellac over the entire surface. The old wastebasket will look new and will be a useful decoration for the Christmas season!
- Cut them out, punch a hole through the top, string with yarn, and hang them from the Christmas tree as ornaments.

Follow-Up Activity

1. Let the students share ideas from their activity pages.

Name _____

USE THOSE CHRISTMAS CARDS!

How many different things can you think of to do with used Christmas cards?

1. _____
   _____

2. _____
   _____

3. _____
   _____

4. _____
   _____

5. _____
   _____

6. _____
   _____

7. _____
   _____

8. _____
   _____

More ideas? Continue writing them on the back of this page or on a separate sheet of paper. Then circle the ideas you like best.

Teaching Suggestions for
DESIGN A COMMEMORATIVE STAMP

Creative-Thinking Objectives

Originality
Elaboration

Activity Introduction

1. Distribute duplicated copies of the activity page.
2. Read aloud the instructions on the page.
3. Have on hand some examples of commemorative stamps to pass around for students to examine, or ask students to bring some to class.
4. Encourage pupils to use colored pencils, crayons, and/or colored markers to add color to their stamps.
5. Let pupils work on the activity independently during class time.

Sample Student Responses

(They will vary greatly.)

Follow-Up Activities

1. *Bulletin Board Display:* Have the students cut out their stamps and display them on a bulletin board so that they can see and enjoy one another's ideas.
2. *Letter Writing:* Have each student write a letter to the Postmaster General of the United States persuading him to accept the commemorative stamp for distribution.

Name _____

Commemorative stamps are postage stamps with pictures and identifying words to honor some special person, place, thing, occupation, skill, or other thing or idea. Think of some special person, place, or thing you feel deserves to be recognized by having a commemorative stamp designed for it. Select the subject with care and specific reasoning.

Now design the stamp! An enlarged stamp outline has been provided below. Do your preliminary sketching and planning on another piece of paper, then draw the final version on this page. Be sure to include the subject being commemorated, a word or two describing the subject, and the postage price.

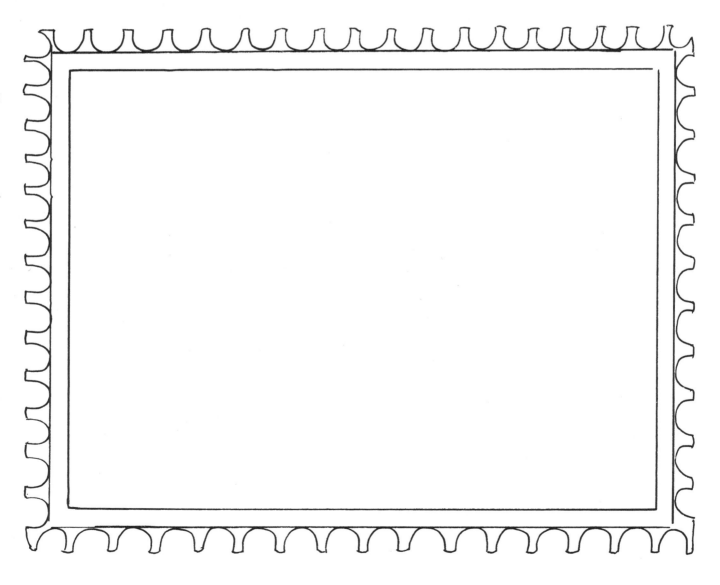

Teaching Suggestions for
TRULY A BEST FRIEND!

Creative-Thinking Objectives

Fluency
Flexibility
Elaboration (Follow-Up Activity 2)

Activity Introduction

1. Hand out duplicated copies of the activity page.
2. Have a volunteer read aloud the activity instructions on the page.
3. Let students work in pairs to develop their lists of ideas. As the students are working, walk slowly among them pausing here and there to make appreciative comments about the ideas the students are generating. Comments such as, "What good ideas!", "I like your thinking!", and "Wow! What an excellent list you've developed already!" help keep students motivated and continuing to stretch their imaginations for more ideas.

Sample Student Responses

Things to teach the puppy:
- to bring my school books to me when I'm ready to study
- to entertain my baby sister
- to guard the house
- to pull the covers over me when I fall asleep

Things you can do together:
- Go hunting
- Go exploring
- Sleep in the same bed

Follow-Up Activities

1. Let pairs of students volunteer to share some of their favorite ideas from their papers. Explain to the students that they are to share only ideas that are different from those that have already been given. Accept ideas with positive comments. Praise the class for excellent thinking ability.
2. *Creative Writing:* Have each pair of students collaborate to write an original story about a boy or girl and a new puppy. They can use the ideas generated in the activity as a basis for the story. The story can be told in the first person either from the point of view of the boy or girl, or from the point of view of the puppy. It can include dialogue and can be either humorous or serious. The completed stories can be shared by volunteers aloud or displayed on a bulletin board so that the students can enjoy one another's ideas.

Name _____

TRULY A BEST FRIEND!

Imagine that you have just been given a puppy of your own! As you lovingly pet your new puppy, you are excitedly thinking of all the things you can teach your puppy and all the wonderful things you can do together. List them below.

THINGS TO TEACH THE PUPPY	THINGS YOU CAN DO TOGETHER
1. _____	1. _____
2. _____	2. _____
3. _____	3. _____
4. _____	4. _____
5. _____	5. _____
6. _____	6. _____
7. _____	7. _____
8. _____	8. _____
9. _____	9. _____
10. _____	10. _____
11. _____	11. _____
12. _____	12. _____
13. _____	13. _____
14. _____	14. _____
15. _____	15. _____
16. _____	16. _____
17. _____	17. _____
18. _____	18. _____
19. _____	19. _____
20. _____	20. _____

Teaching Suggestions for
NEW YEAR'S RESOLUTIONS

Creative-Thinking Objectives

Fluency
Flexibility
Originality (Follow-Up Activity 2)

Activity Introduction

1. Distribute duplicated copies of the activity page.
2. Read aloud the activity instructions on the page.
3. Encourage the pupils to give serious thought to the resolutions and avoid frivolous responses. Because some of the students' ideas may be rather personal, allow them to keep their papers confidential.
4. Let the pupils complete the activity independently during class time.
5. After the activity has been completed, instruct the pupils to put a circle around each of the six resolutions they like best.
6. Then ask them to put a star to the left of each resolution they think no one else would have thought of.

Sample Student Responses

- I resolve not to tease the girl who sits in front of me.
- I resolve to make only complimentary comments about the cafeteria food.
- I resolve to remember to scrape the mud off my shoes before going into the house.

Follow-Up Activities

1. Let students volunteer to share some of their favorite resolutions.
2. Divide the class into groups. Have one group work together to prepare a list of humorous resolutions they think the principal should make. Have another group prepare a list of humorous resolutions for their teacher. Other groups can prepare lists of humorous resolutions for the school cooks, for school bus drivers, for parents, for babysitters, and for other people they know.
3. *Bulletin Board Display:* This display may be put up in December as the new year approaches. Entitle the display "I Resolve . . ." and staple a real New Year's Eve party hat, noisemaker, and streamers to the board, and glue a shower of confetti here and there. Then invite the students to contribute creative New Year's resolutions for famous people (living or dead) or current personalities. Have the students inject a lot of humor and cleverness into their ideas to make them suit the person chosen. You might start them off by putting up the first contribution. Make sure each resolution includes the name of the person for which it is intended.

Name _____

It's that time of year again! Think of 20 realistic New Year's resolutions you could make. Write them below and circle the six you think are best. Place a star by the ones you think no one else would have thought of.

1. _____
2. _____
3. _____
4. _____
5. _____
6. _____
7. _____
8. _____
9. _____
10. _____
11. _____
12. _____
13. _____
14. _____
15. _____
16. _____
17. _____
18. _____
19. _____
20. _____

HAPPY NEW YEAR

Teaching Suggestions for
MY NEIGHBORHOOD
GETS BETTER AND BETTER!

Creative-Thinking Objectives

Fluency
Flexibility
Originality
Elaboration (Follow-Up Activity 2)

Activity Introduction

1. Distribute duplicated copies of the activity page.
2. Read aloud the activity instructions on the page.
3. Let the pupils work on the activity independently during class time.

Sample Student Responses

Ideas for improving the appearance of my neighborhood:
- Plant more trees in the yards of the neighborhood.
- Clean up the vacant lot and mow it regularly.

Other ways my neighborhood could be improved:
- Build a public swimming pool in our neighborhood.
- Place bus shelters at some corners so people don't have to wait for the bus in the cold wind.

Follow-Up Activities

1. Let pupils volunteer to share ideas from their papers.
2. *Editorial Writing:* Using the ideas from their activity pages, have each student write a newspaper editorial proposing ways to improve their neighborhood. Each suggestion used in the editorial should be clearly stated and elaborated upon to make a persuasive and effective article. Students may wish to examine some real editorials as models before they begin this assignment.

Name _____

My Neighborhood Gets Better And Better!

Think about your neighborhood. What could be done to improve its appearance? What could be done to improve it in other ways? Write your realistic ideas below and use the back of this page if you need more room.

IDEAS FOR IMPROVING THE APPEARANCE OF MY NEIGHBORHOOD:

1. _____
2. _____
3. _____
4. _____
5. _____
6. _____
7. _____
8. _____
9. _____

OTHER WAYS MY NEIGHBORHOOD COULD BE IMPROVED:

1. _____
2. _____
3. _____
4. _____
5. _____
6. _____
7. _____
8. _____
9. _____

Teaching Suggestions for
NEW USES FOR EVERYDAY OBJECTS II

Creative-Thinking Objectives

Fluency
Flexibility
Originality

Activity Introduction

1. Distribute duplicated copies of the activity page.
2. Read aloud the activity instructions on the page.
3. To get ideas flowing, give the pupils two or three minutes to think of a couple different and unusual, but *practical*, uses for a clothesline. Then let pupils volunteer to share some of those ideas.
4. Have the pupils complete the activity independently during class time.

Sample Student Responses

Glass jar:
- Paperweight
- Vase
- Weighted doorstop

Follow-Up Activities

1. Let students volunteer to share favorite ideas from their papers for each object. As the ideas are given, list them on the chalkboard.
2. *Poster and Table Display:* Have each student choose his or her favorite new use for an everyday object and develop a poster illustrating and describing it. Students should use colored pencils, crayons, or colored markers to create a lively poster. Some students may wish to give a demonstration speech of the new use for the object and use the poster in the speech.

Name _____

NEW USES FOR EVERYDAY OBJECTS II

Think of 12 unusual but *practical* new uses for each object below. Really stretch your imagination!

A GLASS JAR:

1. _____
2. _____
3. _____
4. _____
5. _____
6. _____
7. _____
8. _____
9. _____
10. _____
11. _____
12. _____

A FLY SWATTER:

1. _____
2. _____
3. _____
4. _____
5. _____
6. _____
7. _____
8. _____
9. _____
10. _____
11. _____
12. _____

SHOELACES:

1. _____
2. _____
3. _____
4. _____
5. _____
6. _____
7. _____
8. _____
9. _____
10. _____
11. _____
12. _____

A BOTTLE OPENER:

1. _____
2. _____
3. _____
4. _____
5. _____
6. _____
7. _____
8. _____
9. _____
10. _____
11. _____
12. _____

Teaching Suggestions for
THE BEST THINGS IN LIFE ARE . . .

Creative-Thinking Objectives

Fluency
Flexibility

Activity Introduction

1. Distribute duplicated copies of the activity page.
2. Have a volunteer read aloud the directions on the page.
3. Ask the pupils to give serious thought as they develop their list of ideas of things they most appreciate in life.
4. Provide class time for the pupils to work on the activity page.

Sample Student Responses

- The beauty of nature
- The excitement of winning a game
- The fun and excitement of the Christmas season
- Skiing down a snow-covered slope on a snowy day

Follow-Up Activities

1. Let the pupils share some of their favorite ideas with the rest of the class.
2. *Bulletin Board Display:* Either enlarge the activity page illustration with an opaque projector or use another appropriate drawing or photo as the centerpiece for the bulletin board. Entitle the board "WHAT ARE THE BEST THINGS IN LIFE?" and invite students to contribute their ideas. The ideas may be neatly written on 4" × 6" pieces of colored construction paper or be illustrated with a caption, or consist of a magazine photo with a caption. Students may sign their contributions if they wish.

Name _____

The Best Things In Life Are...

There are many, many great things about being alive! List at least 18 of the best things in life.

1. _____
2. _____
3. _____
4. _____
5. _____
6. _____
7. _____
8. _____
9. _____
10. _____
11. _____
12. _____
13. _____
14. _____
15. _____
16. _____
17. _____
18. _____

Teaching Suggestions for
DESIGN A SCIENCE BULLETIN BOARD

Creative-Thinking Objectives

Originality
Elaboration

Activity Introduction

1. Hand out duplicated copies of the activity page.
2. Read aloud the instructions on the page.
3. Encourage the students to give careful thought to the bulletin boards they are designing. The board may display any aspect of science, but should be well researched and teach something in an interesting way.
4. Explain to the pupils that some of their bulletin board ideas will be selected for use in the classroom during the year.

Sample Student Responses

(They will vary greatly.)

Follow-Up Activities

1. Collect the activity papers and display them so the pupils can see and appreciate one another's ideas.
2. *Bulletin Board Displays:* At various times during the school year, choose a student-created science bulletin board for display. Have the student who created the board help in its preparation and sign his or her name in the lower corner of the board.

Name _____

Design A Science Bulletin Board

Teachers often develop attractive bulletin boards to emphasize an aspect of something being studied. Now it's your turn! Design an attractive and interesting bulletin board that teaches something in the area of science. Be sure to research your scientific facts and to give your board a title. Sketch the board on a piece of scrap paper, then draw your final board below.

Teaching Suggestions for
TWENTY QUESTIONS ON HONEY

Creative-Thinking Objectives

Fluency
Elaboration (Follow-Up Activity 2)

Activity Introduction

1. Hand out duplicated copies of the activity page.
2. Have a volunteer read the activity instructions on the page.
3. Let pupils brainstorm together three or four question possibilities.
4. Ask pupils to think of and write 20 or more new and different questions for which the answer could be HONEY.

Sample Student Responses

- What is found in honeycomb?
- What sweet golden substance tastes delicious on biscuits?
- What do bees make from nectar?

Follow-Up Activities

1. Let pupils volunteer to share aloud some of their favorite questions from their papers. Respond to student ideas with accepting and appreciative comments.
2. *Creative Writing:* Have each student use ideas from his or her activity sheet as the basis for an original poem on *honey*. The poem may or may not rhyme and may be serious or humorous. The completed poetry may be shared aloud by volunteers.

Name _____

Twenty Questions on Honey

What does a bear like to eat? The answer is: *honey*! Write 20 more questions below for which the answer is honey. Use the back of this page if you need more room.

1. _____
2. _____
3. _____
4. _____
5. _____
6. _____
7. _____
8. _____
9. _____
10. _____
11. _____
12. _____
13. _____
14. _____
15. _____

16. _____
17. _____
18. _____
19. _____
20. _____

Teaching Suggestions for
NEW USES FOR EVERYDAY OBJECTS III

Creative-Thinking Objectives

Fluency
Flexibility
Originality
Elaboration (Follow-Up Activity 2)

Activity Introduction

1. Distribute duplicated copies of the activity page.
2. Read aloud the activity instructions on the page.
3. Let the pupils complete the activity independently during class time.

Sample Student Responses

Empty plastic detergent bottle:

• Cut the top half off and use the bottom half as a vase

• A squirt gun

Follow-Up Activities

1. Let the pupils volunteer to share favorite ideas from their papers aloud, one category at a time. As each idea is presented, write it on the chalkboard and accept it with sincere approval.
2. *New Uses Illustrations:* Have each student draw a diagram with captions of his or her favorite new use for an everyday object. The completed illustrations may be displayed on a bulletin board.

Name _____

NEW USES FOR EVERYDAY OBJECTS III

Turn on your imagination and think of ten different uses for each object listed below. If the object needs to be altered for use, briefly describe this.

AN EMPTY PLASTIC DETERGENT BOTTLE:

1. _____
2. _____
3. _____
4. _____
5. _____
6. _____
7. _____
8. _____
9. _____
10. _____

A SOCK:

1. _____
2. _____
3. _____
4. _____
5. _____
6. _____
7. _____
8. _____
9. _____
10. _____

Poster and Bulletin Board Ideas

225

STRETCH YOUR BRAINPOWER...

THINK CREATIVELY!

229

CREATIVE THINKERS NEVER RUN OUT OF IDEAS!

USE YOUR

BRAINSTORM-ABILITY

NO PROBLEM IS TOO TOUGH

FOR A CREATIVE THINKER!

THE IDEAS NEVER STOP COMING WHEN YOU USE YOUR IMAGINATION!

237